David Paul Downs

Recent Works 2009 through 2010

Published by:
Sprocketbox Entertainment 2010

Written and edited by:
Jared Weiss
Lydia Krupinski
Irena Djuric
David Downs

David Downs would like to personally thank the city of Chicago for their support of this project, the writers and editors that contributed to the creation of this book, Sprocketbox Entertainment for the opportunity to be published, and his wife, Lydia for her abundance of encouragement, support, and love.

This project is partially supported by a Community Arts Assistance Program grant from the City of Chicago Department of Cultural Affairs and the Illinois Arts Council, a state agency.

sprocketbox.yolasite.com
davidpauldowns.yolasite.com

Introduction

As humans, we have an innate instinct to express what we experience in the world, and have nurtured this desire since the time of early cave paintings. We create visual representations of moments suspended in time; reporting and recording – but also re-evaluating and re-interpreting what we see. Through art, time is made still. Moments are frozen. Life and all its experiences, external and internal, are held in place within pigment layered atop stretched canvas.

David Paul Downs reexamines the human habitat, exploring "our civilization's abandoned relics, which have been overcome by time and the forces of nature." Mixing oils, acrylics, inks, and other traditional painting applications with photography and organic compounds – including soil, sand, water, wax and clay – he creates a portal to forgotten artifacts lost in the remains of past human civilizations.

"I am creating monuments out of the discarded," Downs says, describing his work. "I work with subjects that are deteriorating, sometimes due to the force of time, sometimes due to immediate destruction. My inspiration comes from the places where nature and the artificial have merged, both struggling to survive but never achieving harmony. Instead, they pollute, invade, and corrode each other. This is our legacy, seen through the remnants of our past."

"Humankind is waking up and noticing the consequences of our destructive practices on the Earth. Even though new ways are being sought to lessen our detrimental impact on the environment, we are overlooking the evidence of a past that still remains – the ship graveyard, the abandoned dance hall, the bath house washed away by the sea. While I do not expect or promote the removal or preservation of the landmarks I photograph, I am creating a dialogue about the relevance of their existence."

Downs blurs the line between photography and painting. His subjects are represented in large realistic oil paintings derived from his own photographic references. Sometimes the images are directly impregnated into a painting via a polymer-transfer method. The image, painted or transferred, serves to anchor us to a shard of reality, a transient truth, a moment caught in time. The subject of the work inspires Downs' choice of organic materials, which are blended and blurred across the canvas.

Downs states, "I enjoy photographing in black and white because my materials complement the monochomatic color scheme I use. For instance, I use black India ink for its flatness and tinting ability. Acrylic paint is mixed with soil to create a texture that can be cracked or eroded. Soil is also used dry or wet, and is allowed to settle into the painting naturally. Lines of erosion occur when I rush a canvas with water. Sometimes I pour water mixtures onto a canvas and agitate it for days until it dries. I often repeat this process for weeks, experimenting with different combinations of water, soil, and paint. These materials take on tones of warm and cool greys and rich blacks creating an illusion of color and depth."

Although Downs' paintings initially appear as ominous interpretations of reality, they yield a certain luminescence upon closer investigation. They are born from a sense of curiosity and awe. To look at his towering canvasses is to be engulfed in a dreamlike landscape of corroding relics, newly unearthed. Entering this world, we feel the wonder he himself felt as he captured their existence on canvas. But Downs doesn't impose definitions. Instead, he invites each of us to create our own interpretations of these worlds.

This catalog is a documentation of the works of David Paul Downs, created between 2009 and 2010. The pages are intermixed with the artist's own narrative, offering a glimpse into the planning, process, and execution of his work. It is concluded with a recent interview conducted by artist and critic, Jared Weiss, accompanied by photographs of David Paul Downs' studio. We invite you into this world to explore the art of David Paul Downs through this intimate collection that is the first book in our Future Masters series.

-the editors at Sprocketbox Entertainment, November 2010

David Downs
Thoughts and Reflections on Art

Communication above all else, I believe, is responsible for the development of human kind. The complexity of information we are capable of relaying has allowed for our species to thrive and develop like no other on Earth. This being said, I will admit that I have never been a confident conversationalist. In fact, throughout my childhood I was always the awkward quiet kid that kept to himself. As I grew to a young adult, I tried developing this disability into a mystique. Maybe my silence was hiding a deep secret that only a lucky few would be made aware. I'm not sure if anyone bought that idea, but there are surely worse things to be than shy. For all the things I couldn't communicate verbally, and wouldn't make sense to write about, there was always art. With art, I can express ideas beyond words. I can also leave these ideas up for interpretation. It is like sharing a conversation with friends or strangers that somehow becomes intimate. I, through my artwork, and you as the viewer, bring to this conversation very personal thoughts. I can tell you as much as I can through a work but it is really your interpretation, constructed from your experiences, that prevails. Of course if the art work is successful, it will persuade you to adapt my ideas as your own. It becomes a symbiotic relationship. The life of an artist can be a lonely venture. You spend hours away from the world, intentionally stealing yourself away to a place that exists in your mind and in your studio. Being an active, showing artist is one of the few ways to let others into this place. Art, as I mentioned earlier, is a conversation. When the work is not seen, it is a one way conversation. You wouldn't want to be caught talking to yourself!

Arco: Mouth of Sacbe
72 in x 96 in
oil, acrylic, clay, honey, coffee grounds, on canvas
David Paul Downs 2010

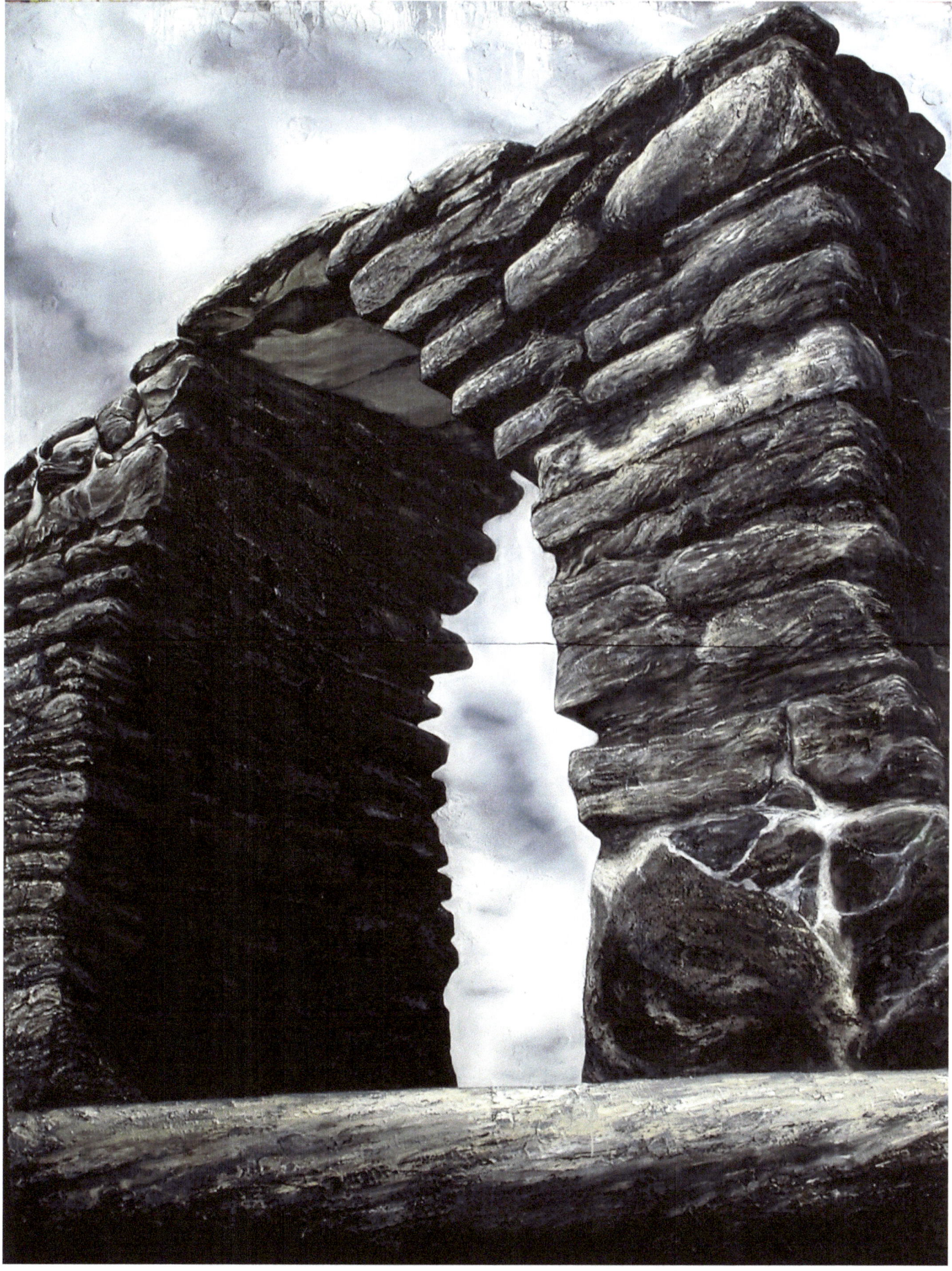

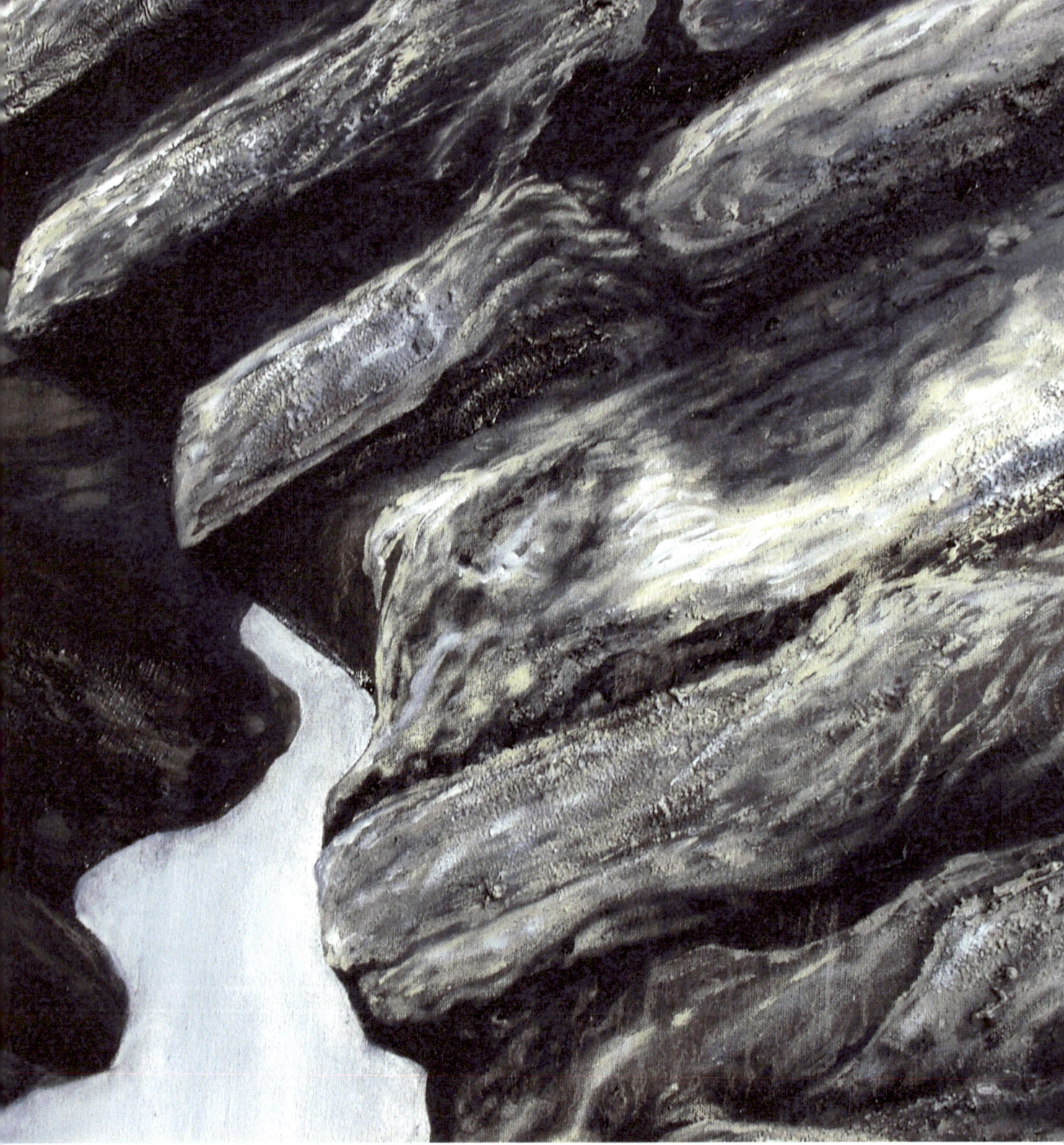

Arco: Mouth of Sacbe
Detail

When I paint, I begin with a very realistic idea. I have a goal in mind as to what I am portraying, the materials I will use and how, and what the final outcome will be. Since a painting may take several weeks or months to finish, these things may change before completion. Also, while the basic notion of the painting is representational, the way I use the materials is sometimes metaphorical. When painting an ancient monument, for example, I try to layer the paint as if I am constructing it. I use thick layers of paint, often mixed with soil or sand to add more weight. I will also research the original materials used to construct the monument to find something I can use with the paint. In "Arco: Mouth of Sacbe" and "Ka`na Nah: House of Ix Chel" from the Xac Be series, I used honey mixed into oil paint and soil. The Mayans who built these structures used honey in the stucco. Other materials like dried, cracking clay is used to describe the idea of fragility, and wax is used to describe transparency. These abstract ideas are conveyed through the properties of the materials. I believe a good painting should have more to experience than what can be absorbed in a single glance. Many great classic painters would create really complex scenarios in their paintings that involved many characters or actions. While I tend to focus on a singular subject or event visually, the larger part of the story is told through the different layers of material. My artworks need to be examined and studied to unlock all the intricacies being expressed.

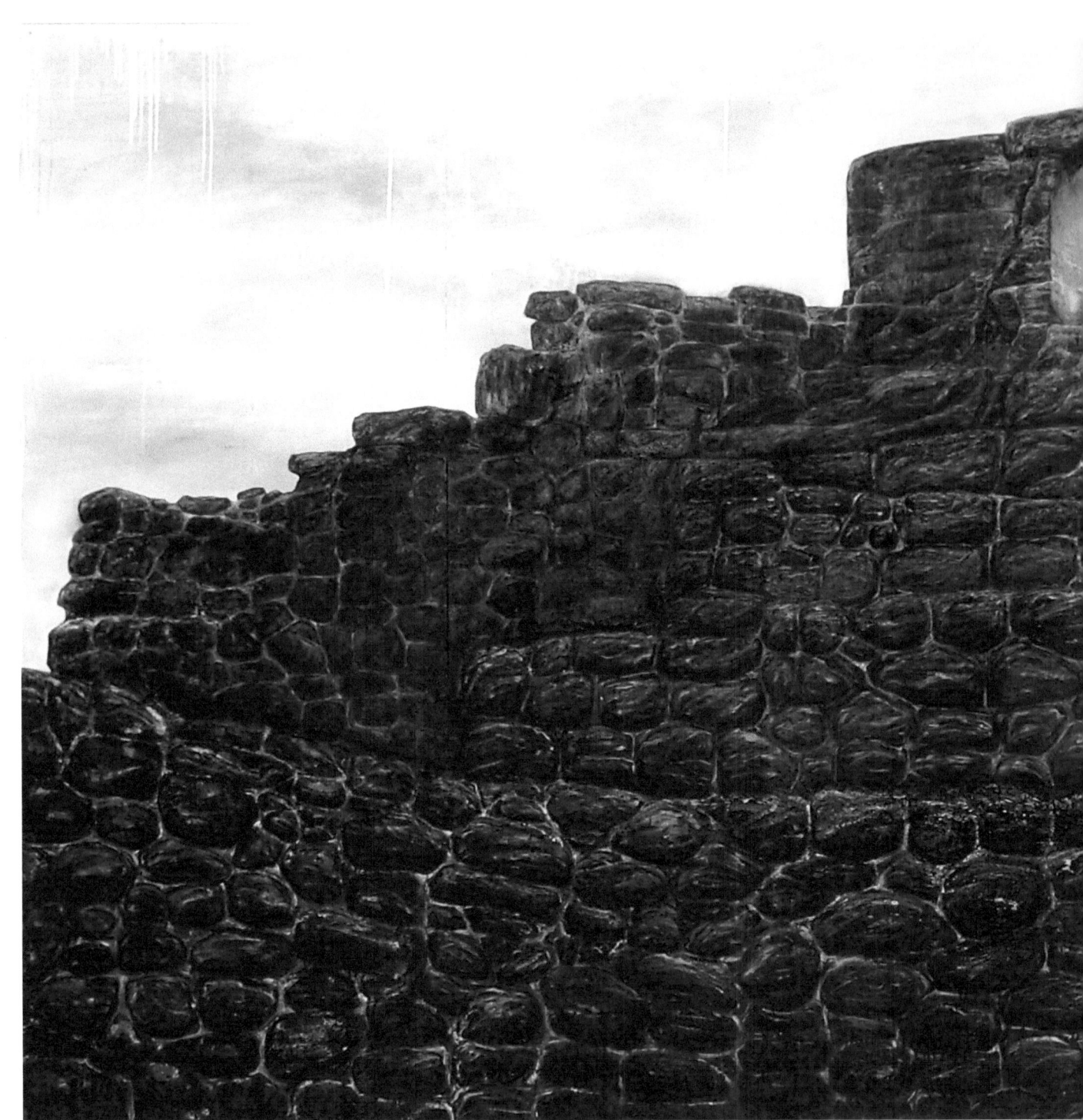

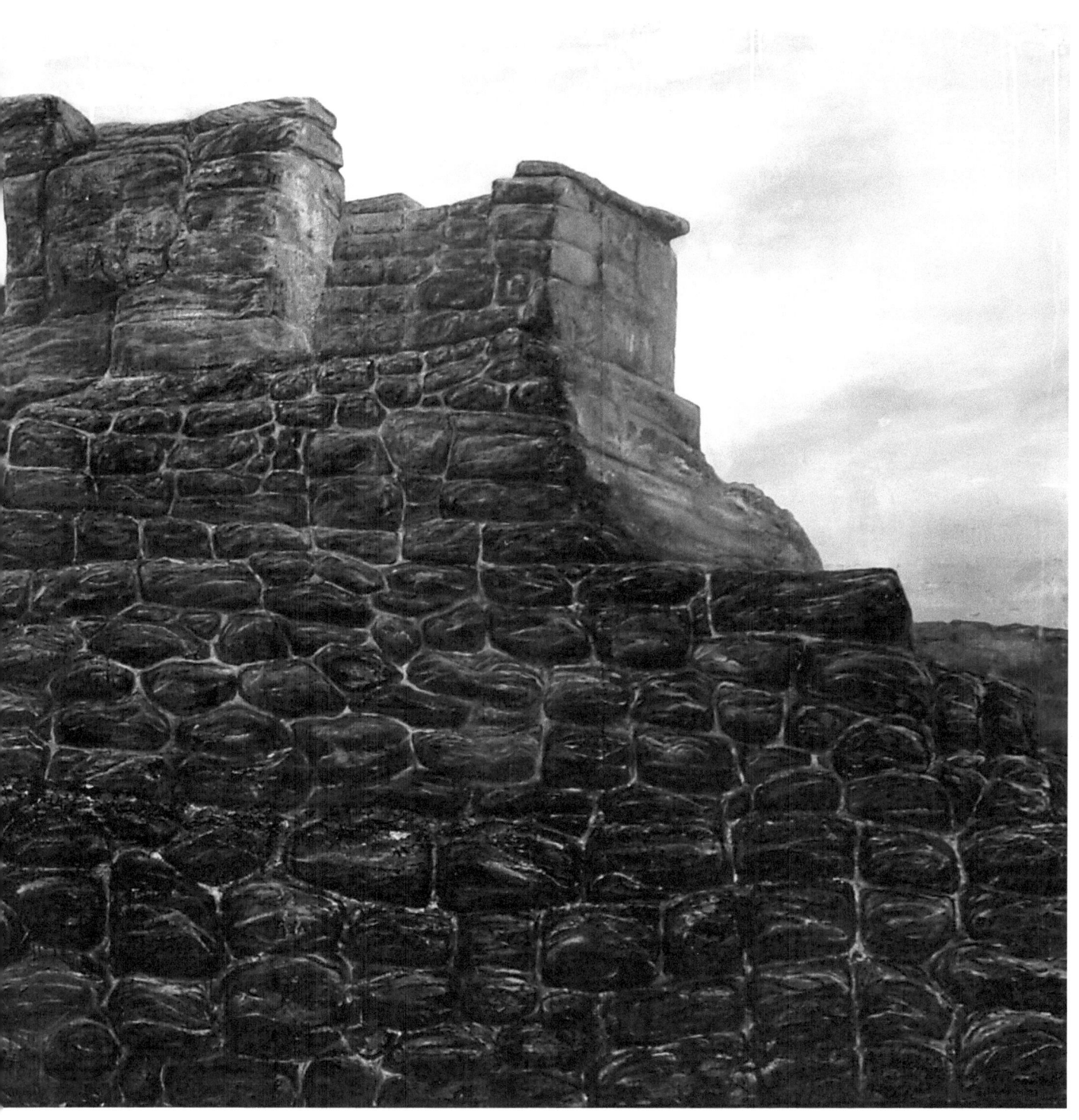

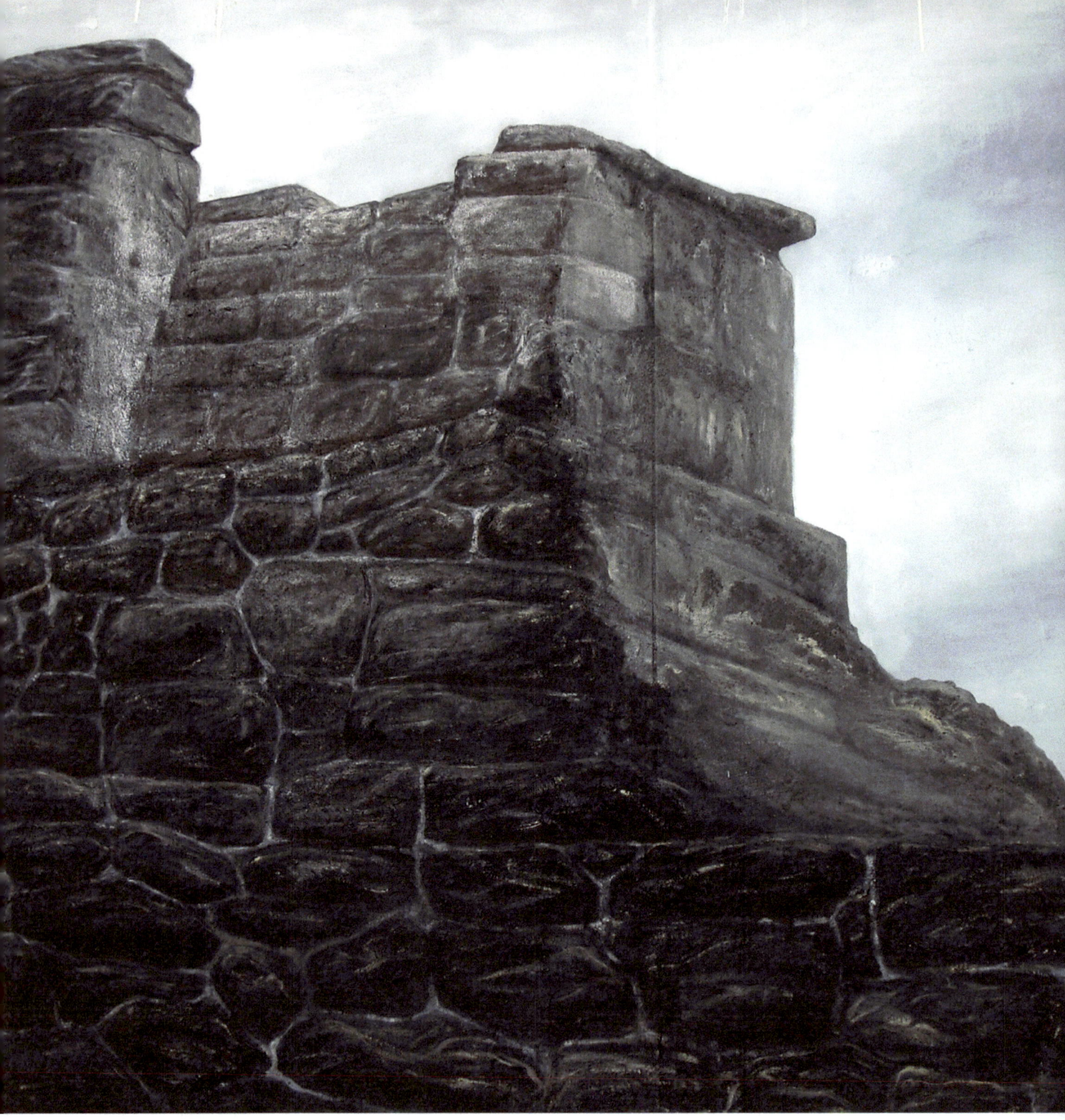

(previous page)
Ka`na Nah: House of Ix Chel
169 in x 84 in
oil, acrylic, sand, clay, honey, coffee, on canvas
David Paul Downs 2010
(this page - detail)

My works are almost always monotone in color scheme. This is largely due to my training in black and white photography. I began to photograph and develop b&w film at the age of 15 and soon assembled my own darkroom to accommodate this. What fascinated me about b&w photographs was the ability to focus on light and shadow. Also, when looking at a photo without color, you were only given a portion of the complete picture. You have to make up the rest in your mind. The color of the light, the sky, the reflections, buildings, trees... you have to fill in the blanks. It is a participatory thing, and I enjoy how it sparks my imagination. I try to bring this into my paintings. By removing color from my pallette I can focus more on the shadows and mood of a piece. Sometimes I add a warm grey to a plane or object to break it away from the cooler greys of everything else. This creates the allusion of color, but is still very unsaturated.

Photographs I've taken sometimes make their way into a painting by a method of image transfer. There are some subjects I feel can be best explained in the media of photography. A photograph is real. I can place this "real" thing into an abstracted environment and it remains unquestionable in the mind. Textures and layers will be added to describe the feeling and atmosphere, giving you more than a photograph would alone. If I choose instead to paint a subject, then I am probably trying to represent the importance of its weight in the work. It is much harder to explain mass in the flatness of a photograph.

Xibalba` be
72 in x 99 in
oil, acrylic, cold wax, muslin, on canvas
David Paul Downs 2010

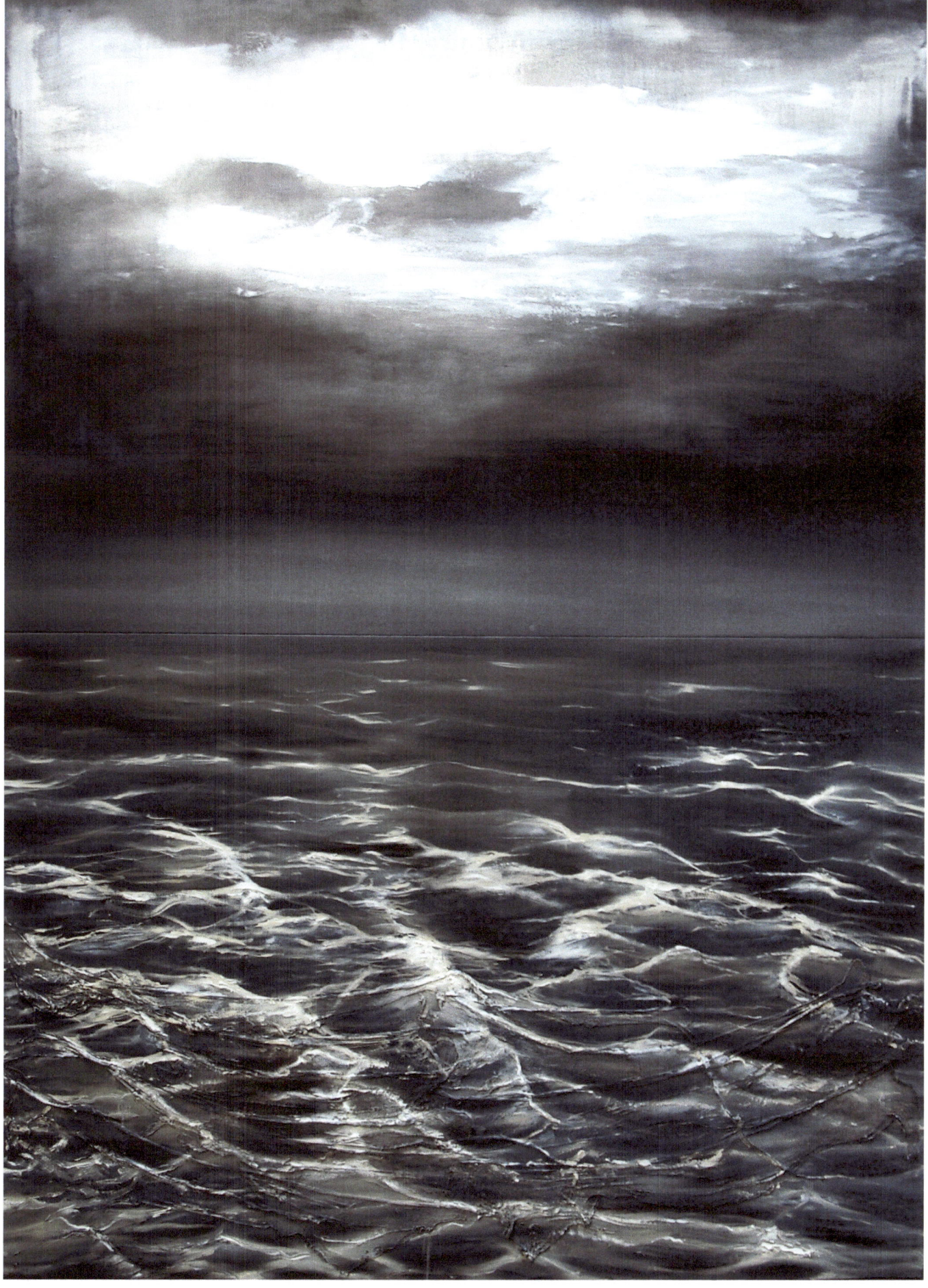

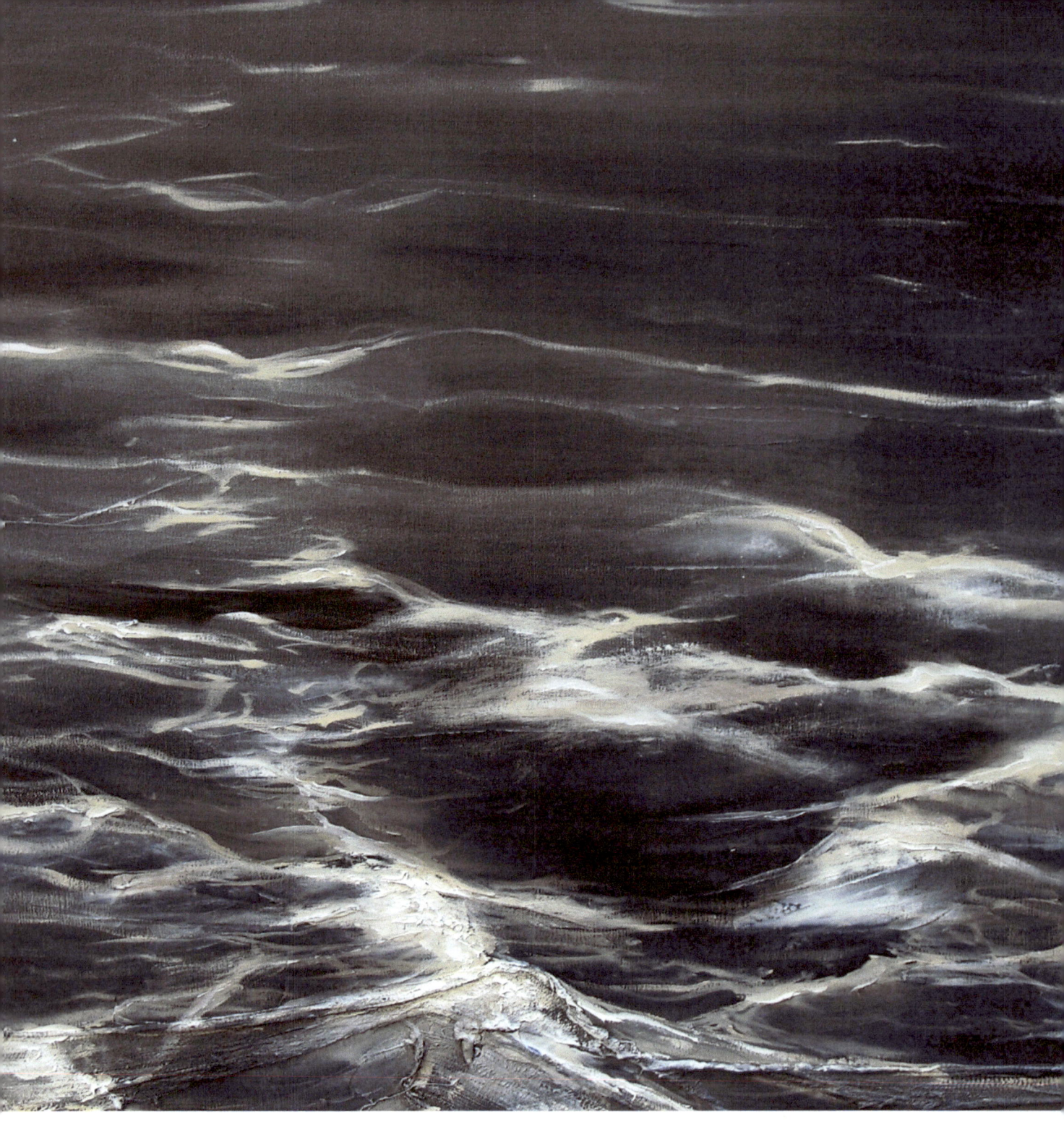

Xibaba` be
(detail)

It remains important to me to constantly reevaluate my direction and process of making art. Many artists are working towards proliferation in their work. They are comfortable and determined to create cohesive works that all fit together. I try to do this in my use of materials and color, but I often feel the need to explore new subjects and directions. When I feel too comfortable with a process, I change something about it. I create new problems to solve. Otherwise I feel the work might become stale. I think art is best when it is in a state of experimentation. Each new series brings new challenges to overcome. This is frustrating to some. They feel that if something is "working" then why try to fix it? At my age, early to mid 30's, I feel far too young to decide what kind of artist I am. That kind of decision shouldn't be made until you've been making art for several decades. Even then, your ideas are still welcome to change. You can reinvent yourself at any time in your life. This is why I switched so much of my recent attention towards painting and away from photography. It is a way to grow in my abilities and techniques. It keeps my work feeling fresh. This coming year will yield even more changes in my work and I am very excited to see the results!

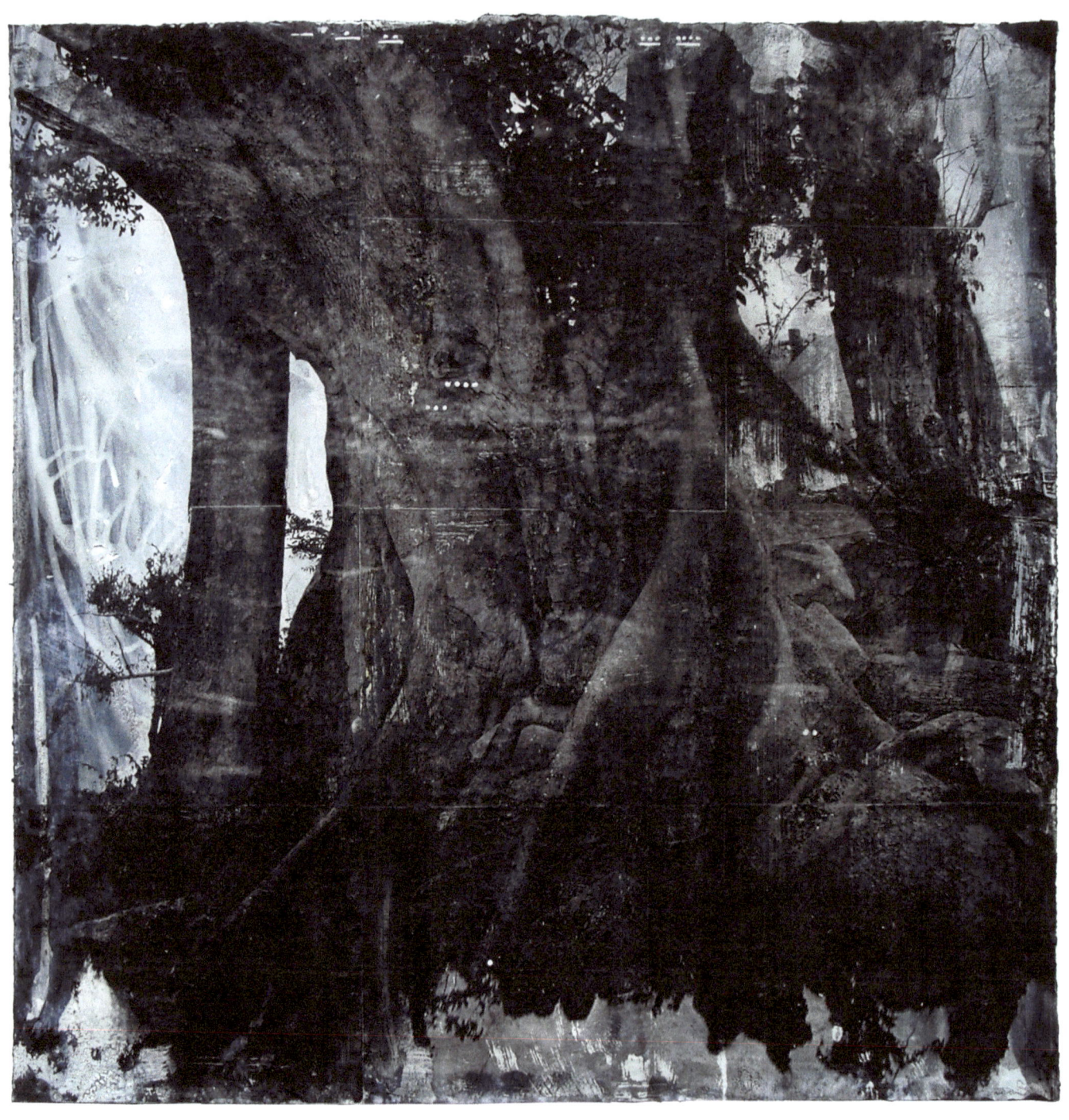

Wakah Chan
30 in x 30 in
oil on photo-polymer emulsion transfer, acrylic on paper
David Paul Downs 2010

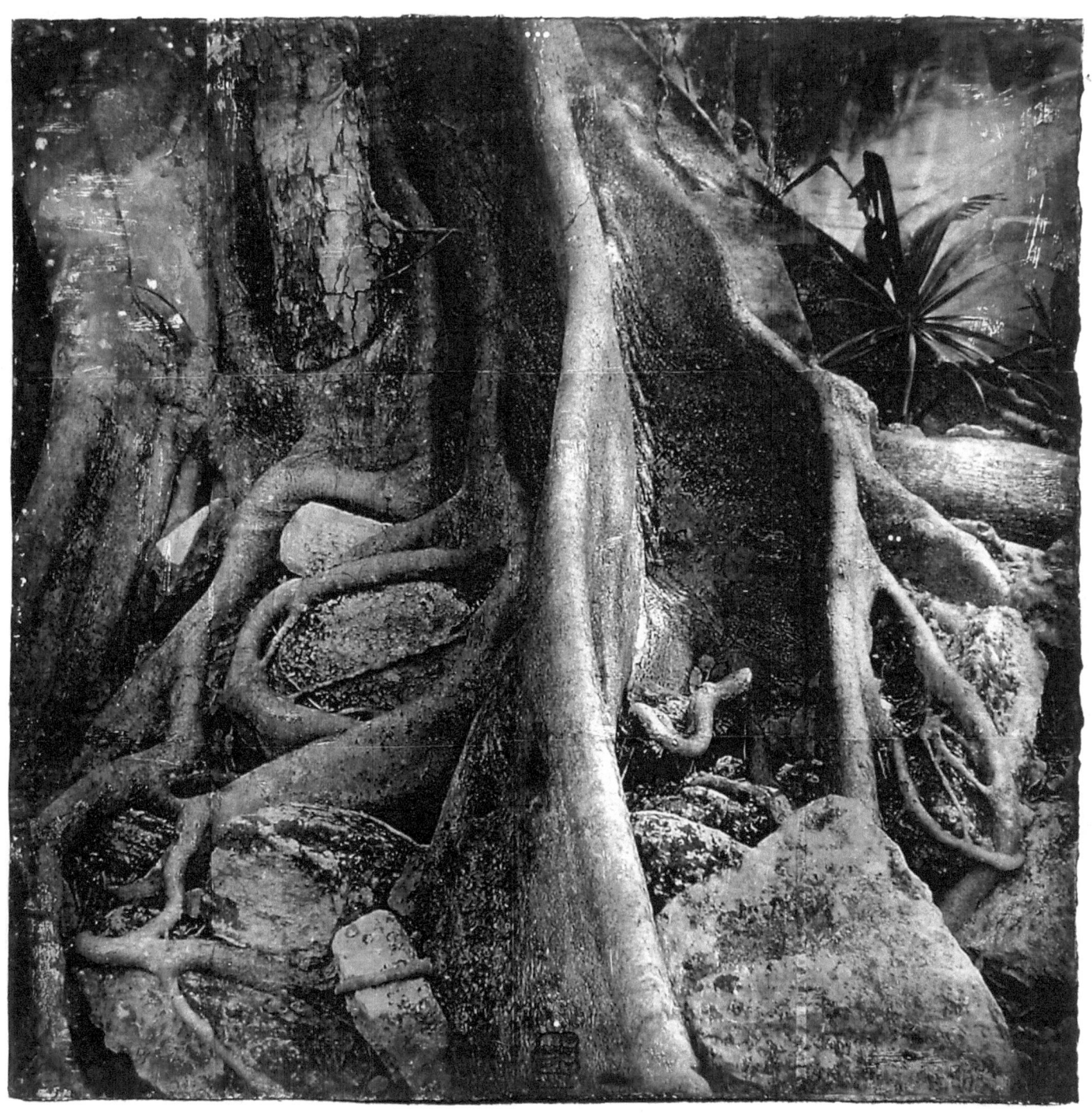

Anchored to Xibalba`
30 in x 30 in
photo-polymer emulsion transfer, acrylic on paper
David Paul Downs 2010

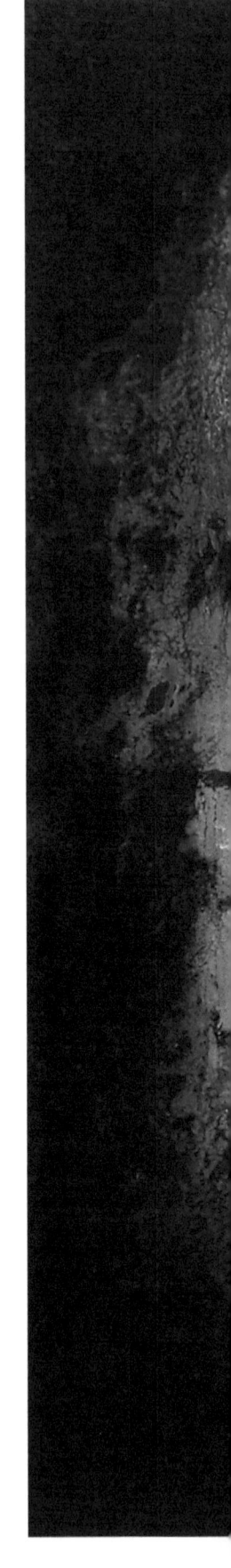

What Is Lost To Lay Adrift
73 in x 73 in
polymer image transfer, soil, coffee grounds,
natural and synthetic bees wax, acrylic, India ink
David Paul Downs 2010

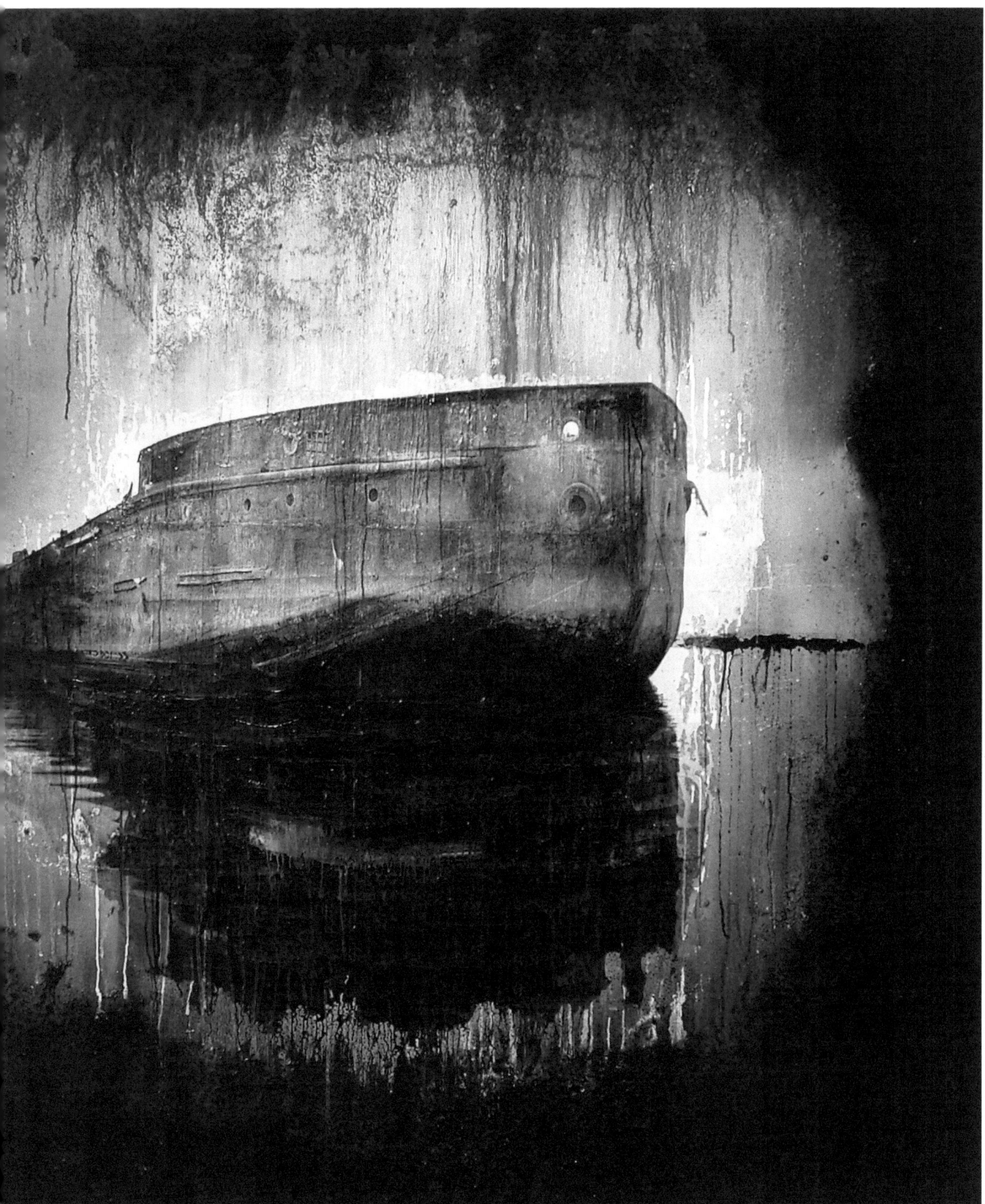

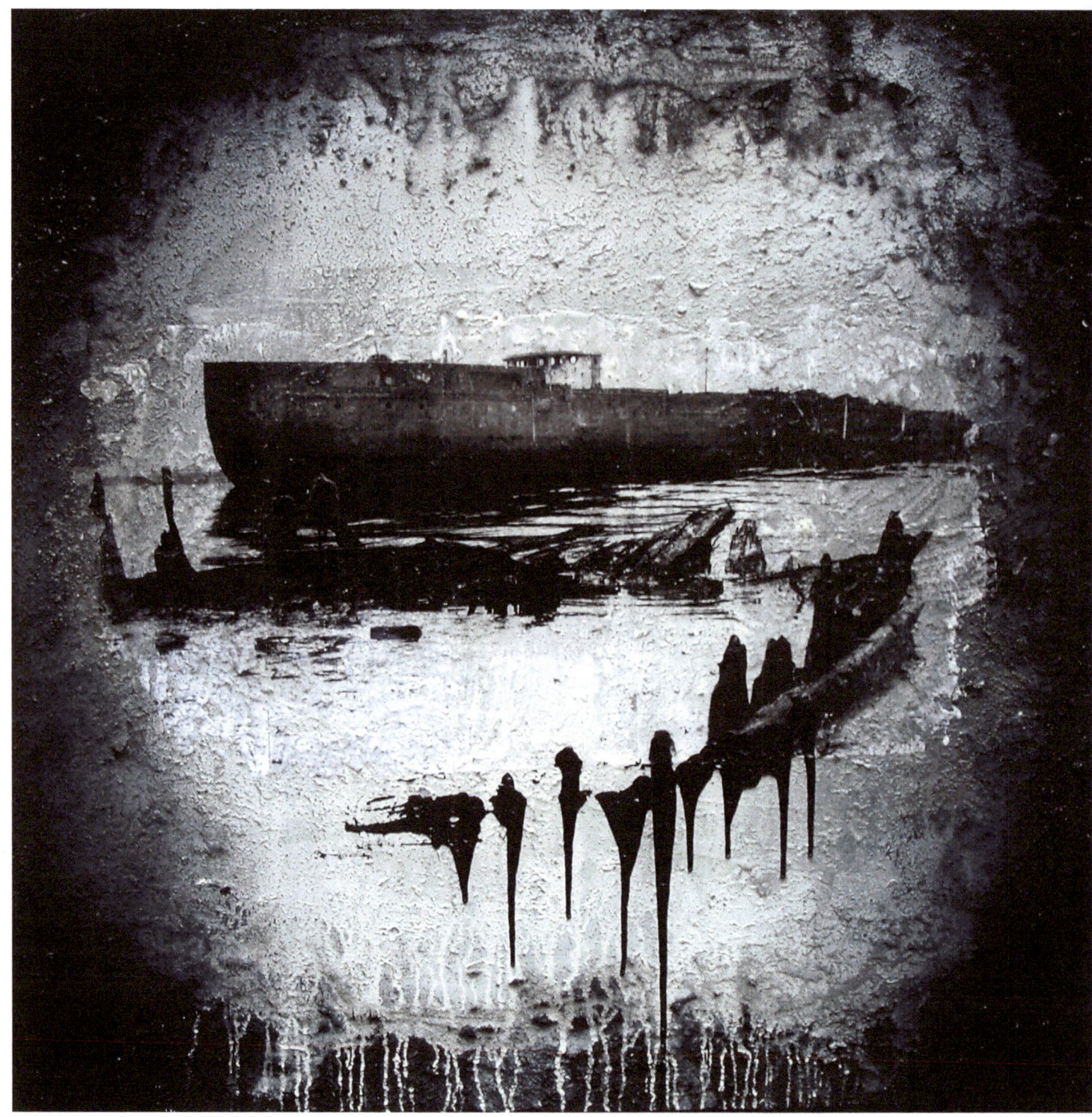

Ghosts of the Sea
49 in x 49 in
polymer image transfer, soil, acrylic, ink, on canvas
David Paul Downs 2010

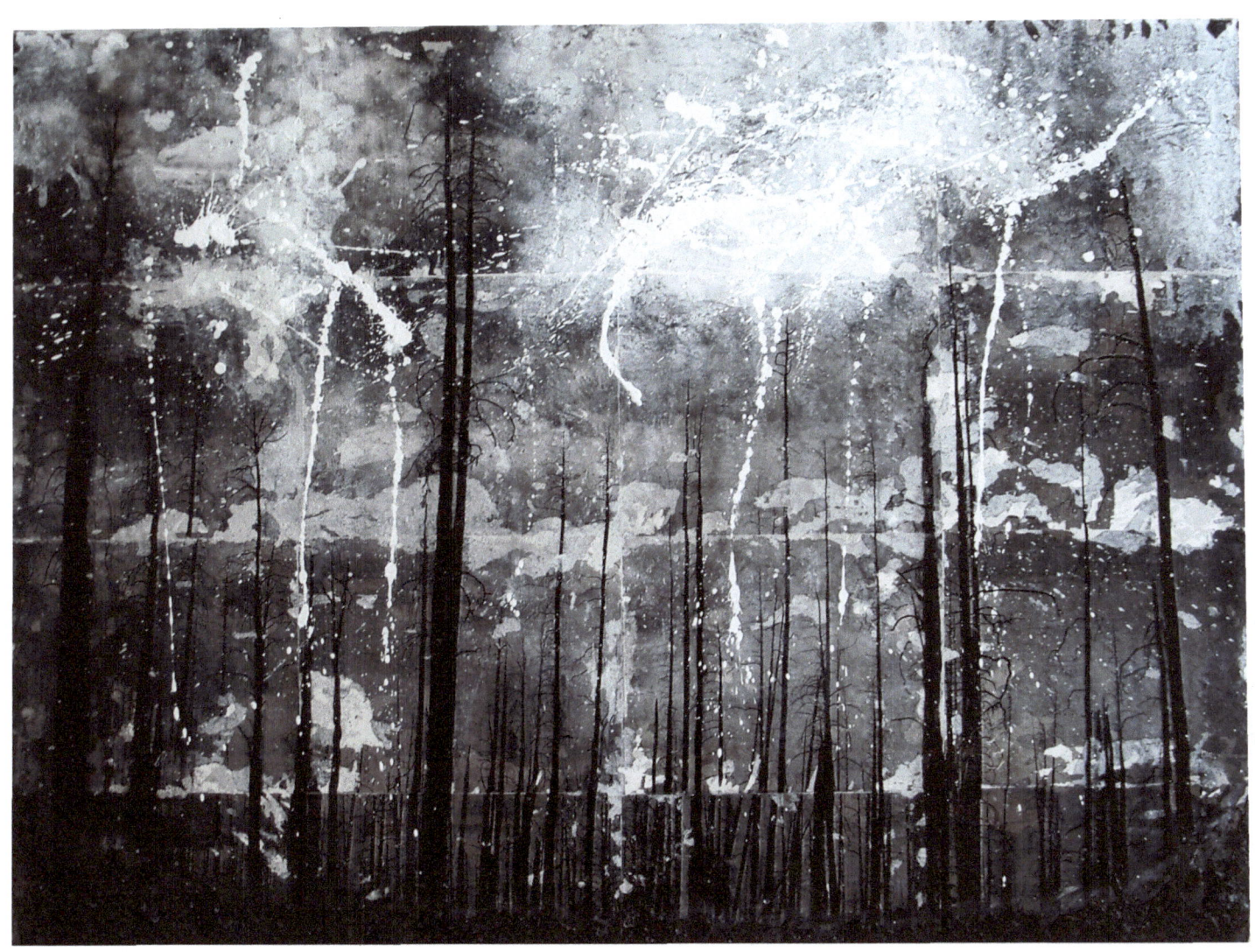

Matchsticks
30 in x 40 in
polymer image transfer, India ink, acrylic, soil, on canvas
David Paul Downs 2009

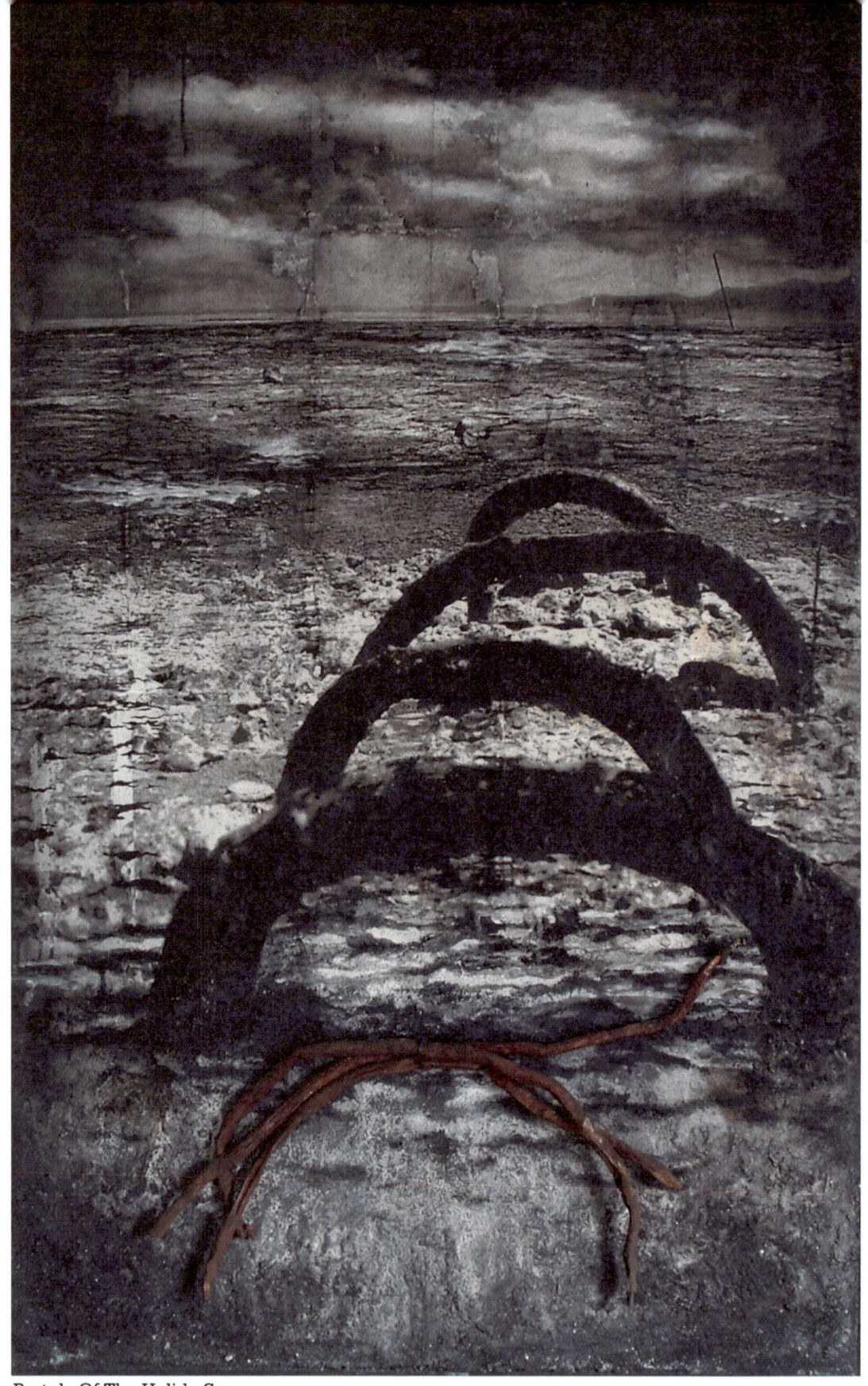

Portals Of The Halide Sea
38 in x 61 in
polymer image transfer, soil, acrylic, India ink, halide, plaster gauze, rust, on canvas
David Paul Downs 2010

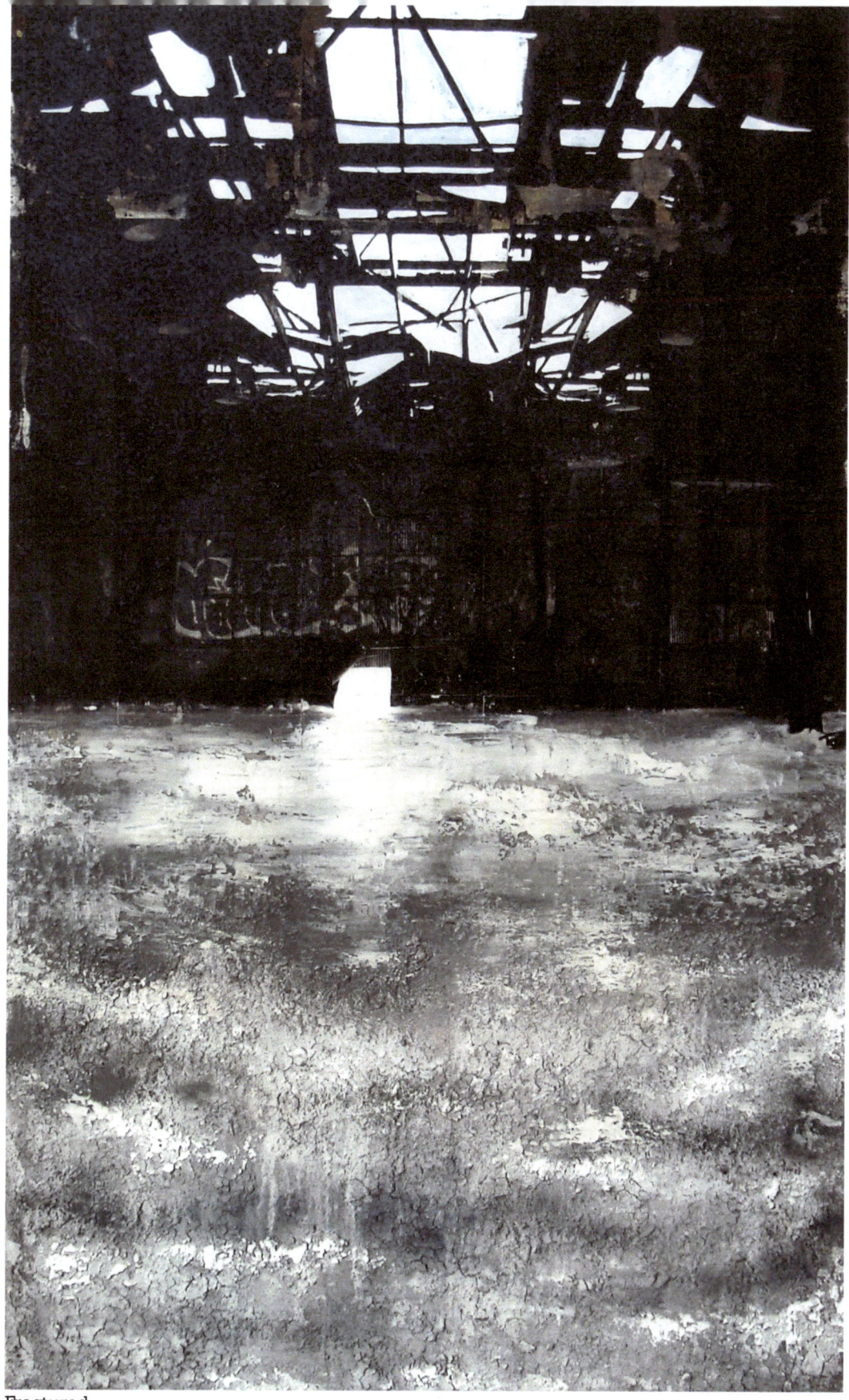

Fractured
36 in x 60 in
polymer image transfer, soil, acrylic, oil, on canvas
David Paul Downs 2009

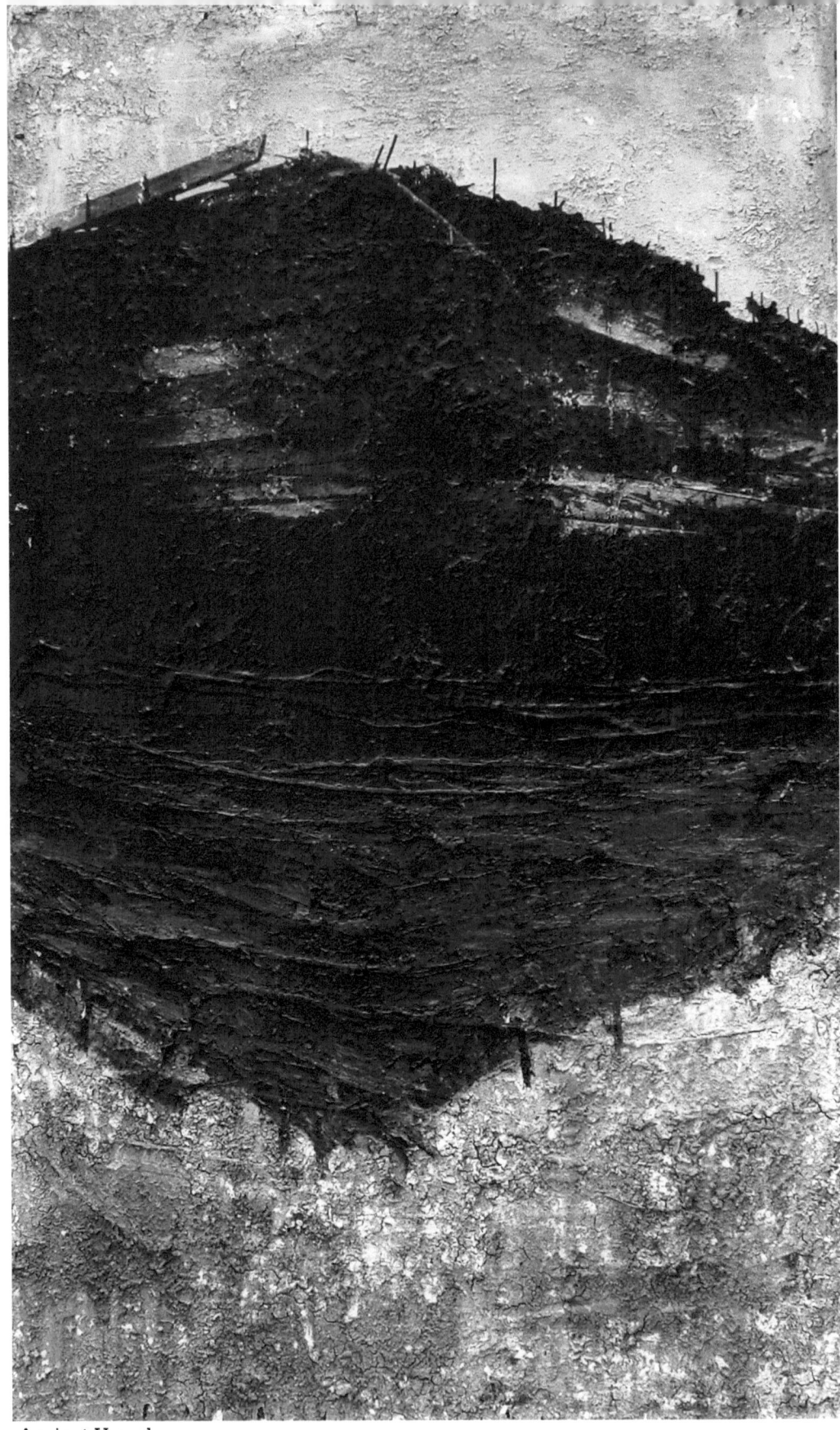

Ancient Vessel
36 in x 60 in
polymer image transfer, soil, acrylic, oil, on canvas
David Paul Downs 2009

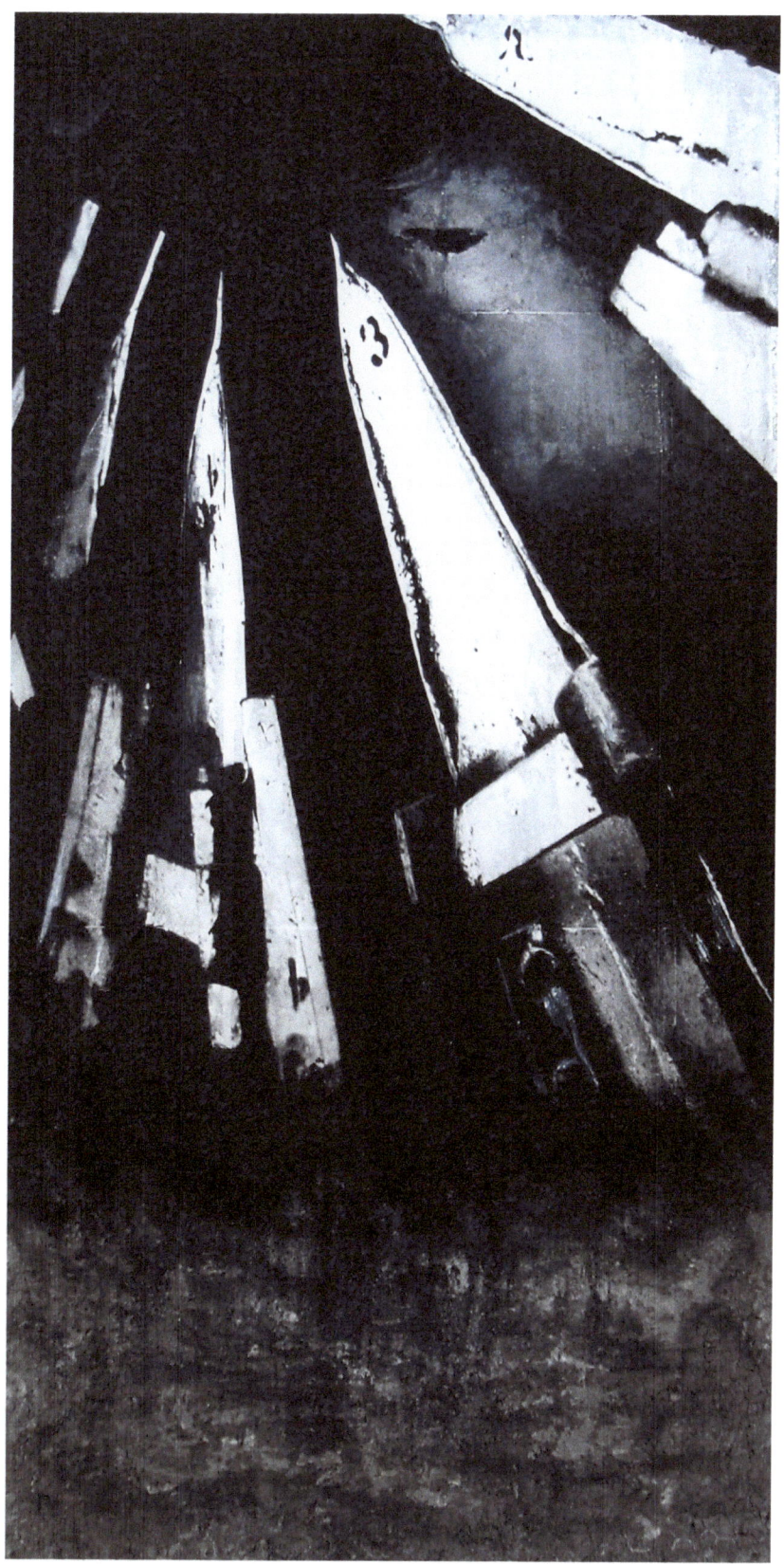

Turbine III
24 in x 48 in
polymer image transfer, soil, acrylic, on canvas
David Paul Downs 2009

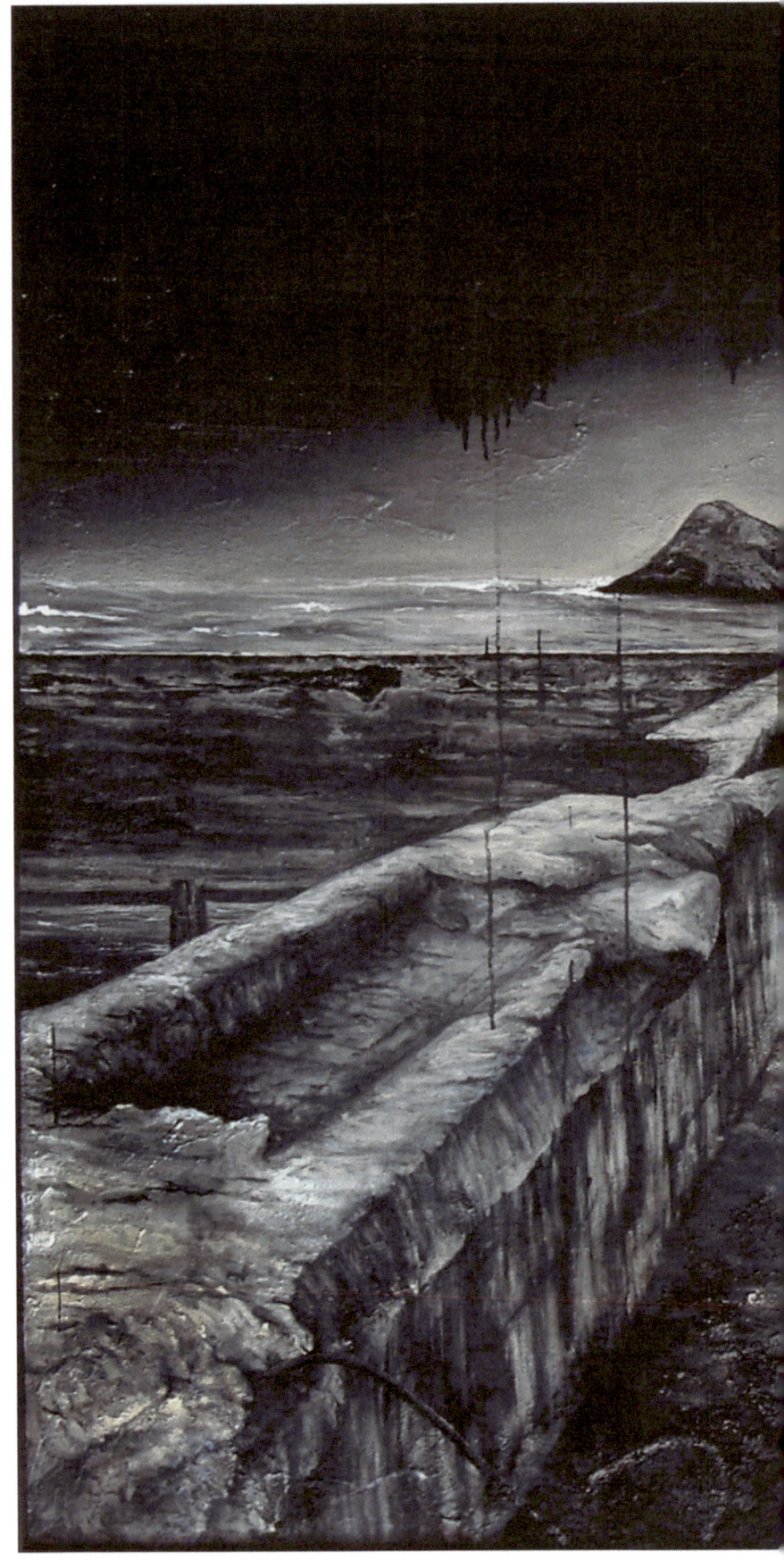

Baptism Of Sutro
74.25 in x 54.5 in
oil, acrylic, India ink, coffee
grounds, terra cotta, on canvas
David Paul Downs 2010

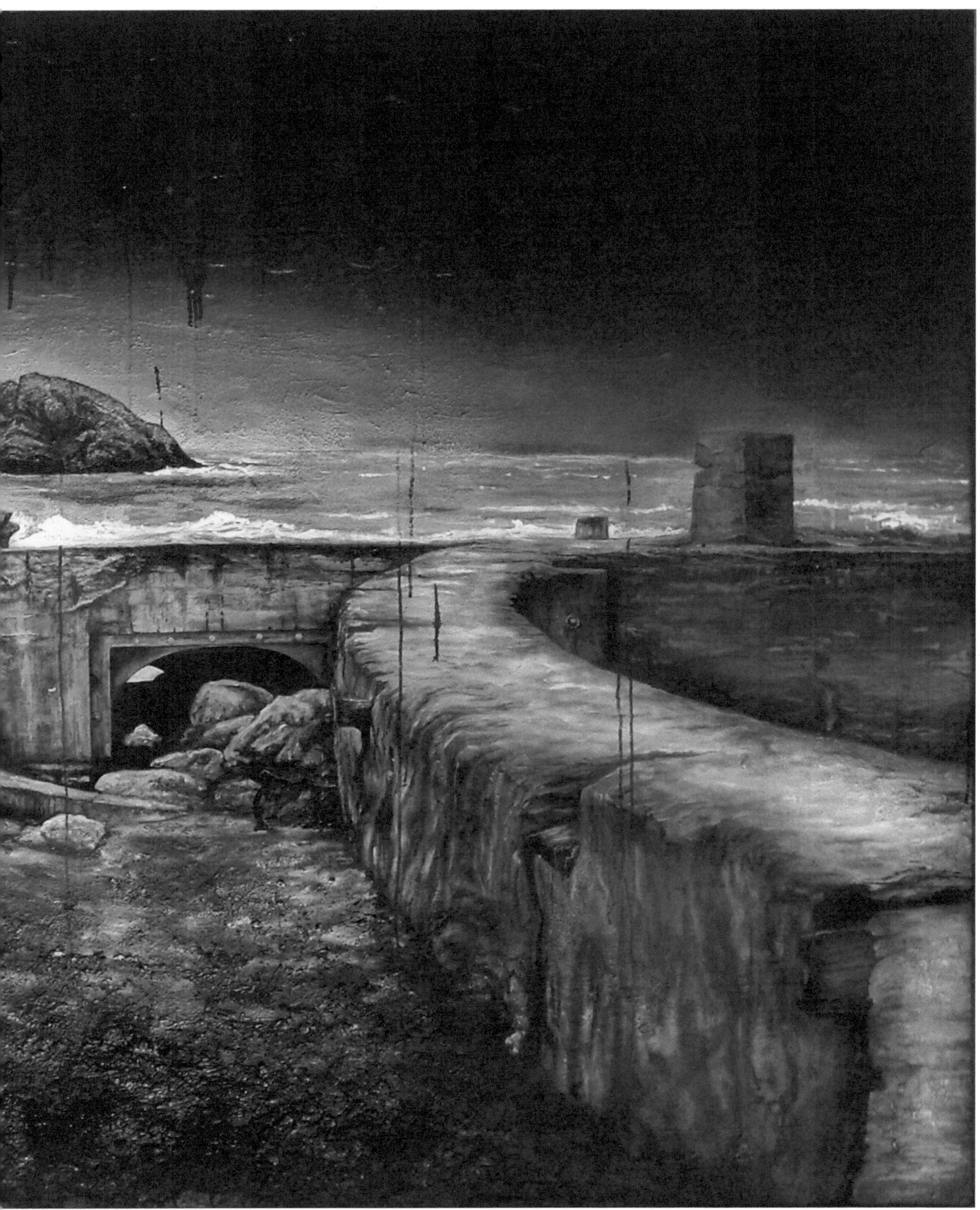

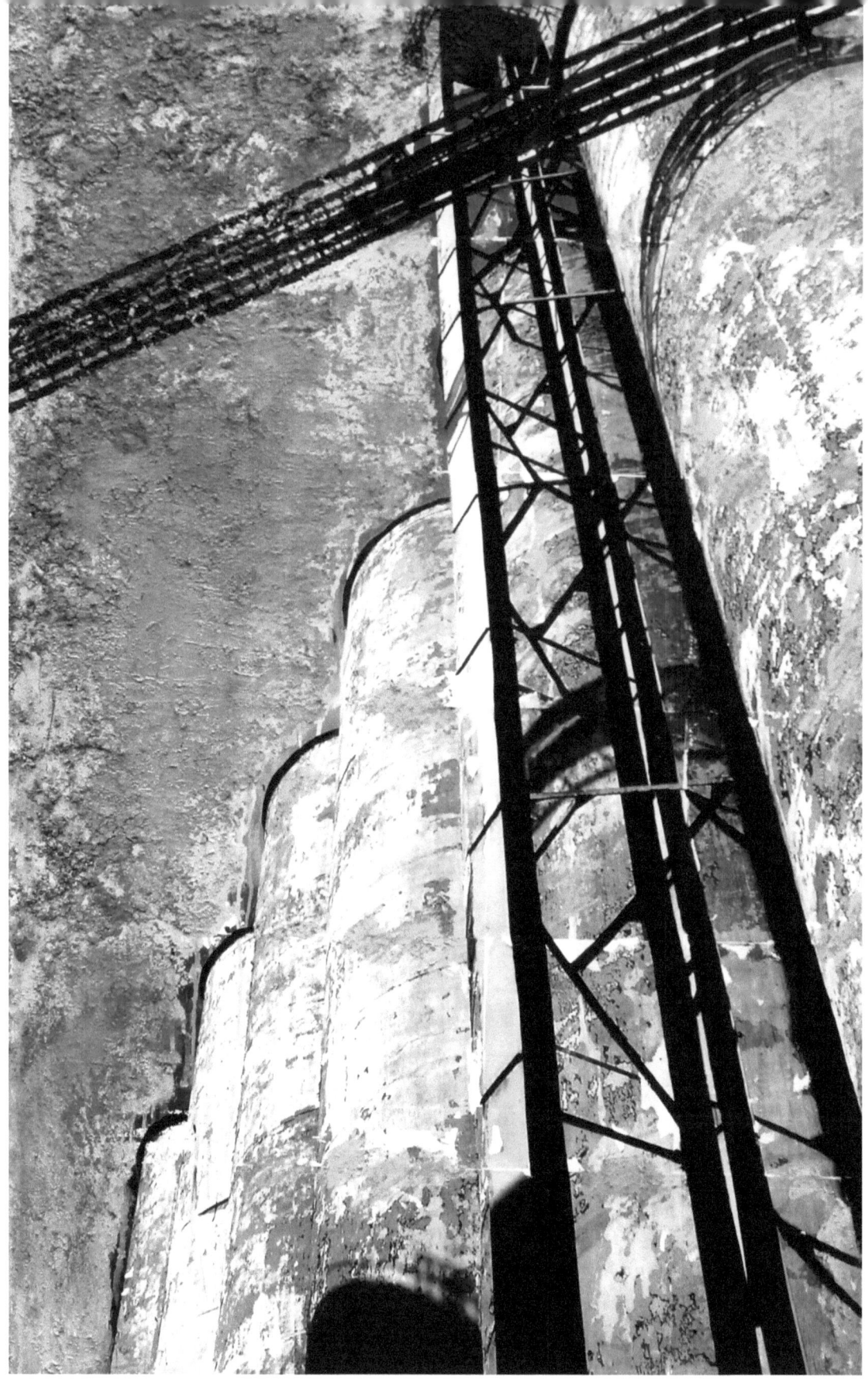

Silos
36 in x 60 in
polymer image transfer, soil, acrylic, on canvas
David Paul Downs 2009

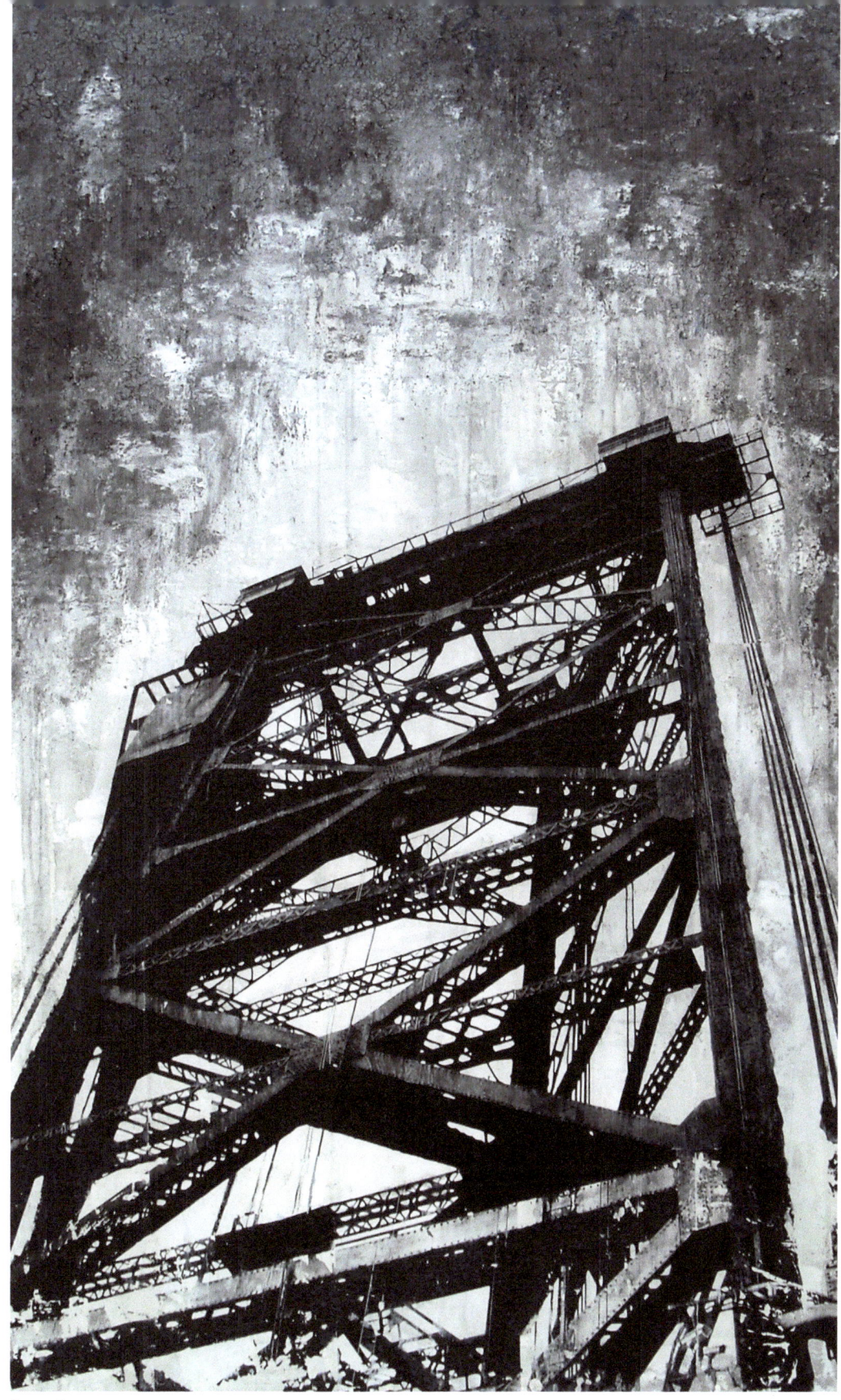

Armature
36 in x 60 in
polymer image transfer, soil, acrylic, on canvas
David Paul Downs 2009

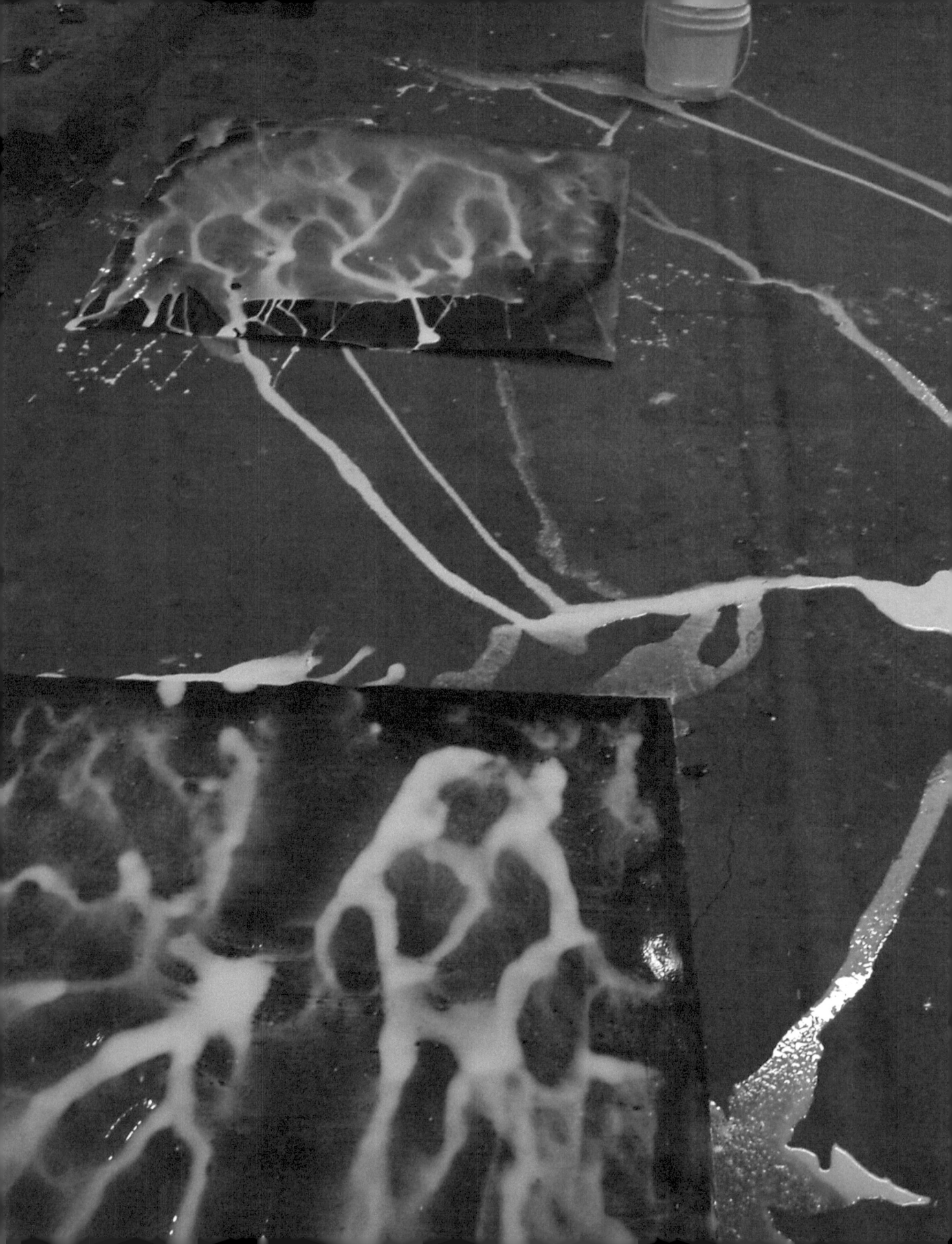

Interview with David Paul Downs
Conducted by: Jared Weiss
November 2010

Jared Weiss: Tell me about Xac Be.

David Paul Downs: Xac Be is the word the ancient Mayans used to describe the Milky Way. It held a lot of precedence in their mythology as a gateway or path to the underworld. I use it as a focal point in my most recent series of works, "Xac Be: the beginning and the end." It represents an unobtainable goal to reach beyond this existence towards something greater. We hear legends of other people doing it and so we believe we can as well. It's the need in all of us to be great, and the disappointment that we often face when we feel we have failed.

JW: And so why are you choosing to paint these monuments?

DPD: The monuments; the ancient ruins from Cozumel and the not-so-ancient ship wrecks, work together to tell a story. The ruins were built to worship the goddess Ixchel. She plays a large part in the beginning and the end of creation. The temples were used for sacrifices made to appeal to her to grant young women an abundance of fertility.

Just as Ixchel can bring new life into existence, she can also wash it away. When the end comes, she will flood the land and wash away all life. The sunken ships can be seen as a metaphor for attempting to survive the flood and avoid an inevitable death. I also use them in reminiscence of the story of the maize god, Hun Hunahpu who ventured to the underworld by canoe though a black rift in the Milky Way.

JW: What happened to him?

DPD: The lords of Xibalba(the Mayan underworld) decapitated Hun Hunahpu and hung his head in a tree.

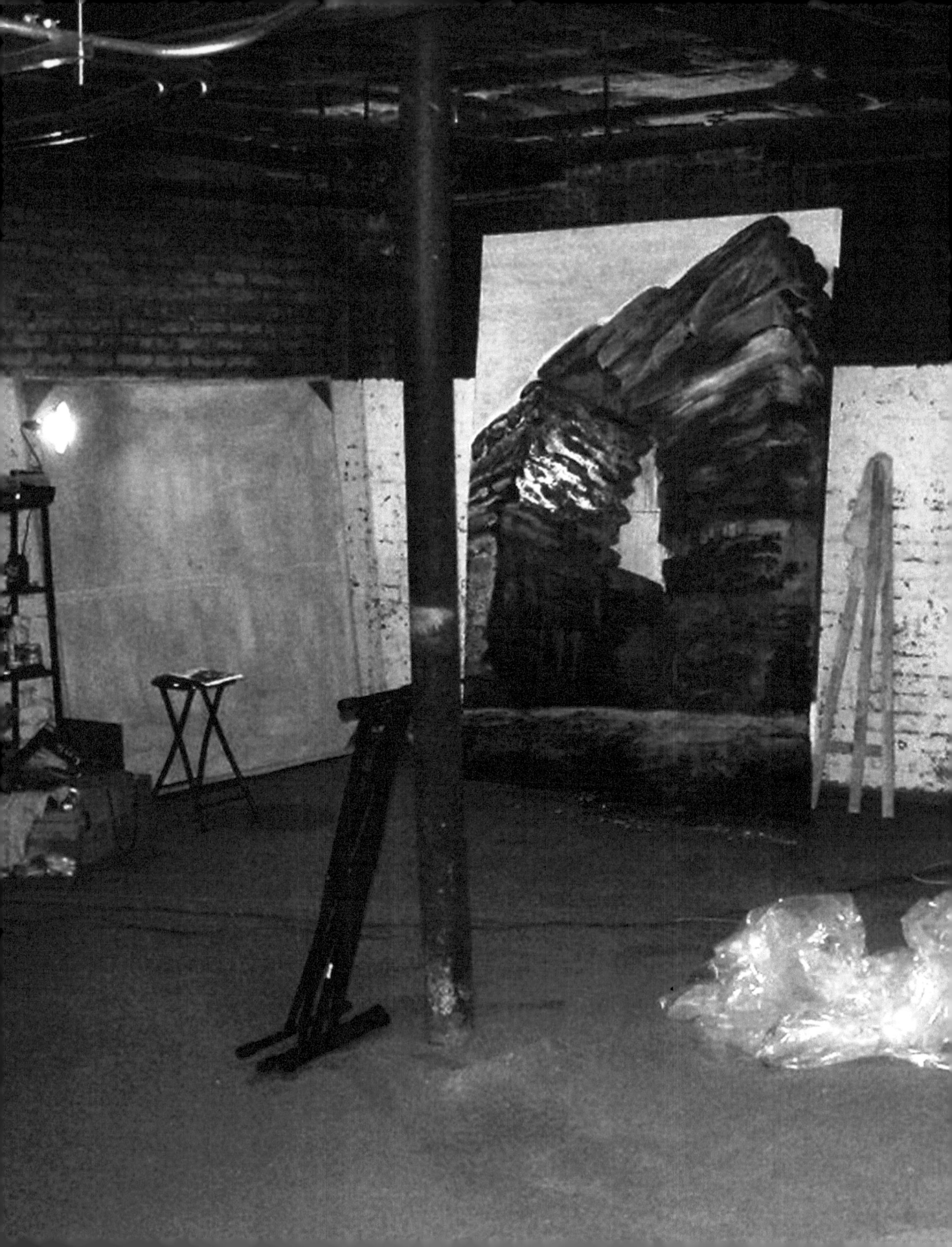

JW: Oh my! because he ventured into the underworld?

DPD: He was tricked into entering Xibalba so he could be made a sacrifice. Coincidentally, it would be Hun Hunahpu's twin sons that would bring about the downfall of Xibalba.

JW: Then what do you think is our relation to this antiquated past?

DPD: Through art, music, literature, architecture and other devices, we have catalogued our existence in an effort to survive beyond death. The things we create and leave behind tell a story of who we were. Everything we know will someday come to an end. Whether we continue to another plane of existence or continue as a legend told by artifacts, we are all just trying to prolong our existence.

In Hun Hunahpu's story, his desires blinded him and he was fooled into an adventure he did not return from. I don't take this as a warning against adventure or following your desires, I do think it's a caution to observe the possible consequences and to prepare yourself against them.

JW: Quite a bit of your work has some type of opening, passageway, or path. Is there a reason for this?

DPD: I think I am attracted to passageways as a beginning to exploration. When you see an open door, you want to move through it. You want to know what is on the other side. I am a very curious person, and when confronted with an invitation such as a path or doorway, my imagination runs wild. I want to discover what lies on and beyond that path. Perhaps I am trying to give that sensation to the viewer of my work.

JW: Why do you paint on such a large scale?

DPD: I paint in whatever size feels right for the subject. I also enjoy being engulfed by a painting.

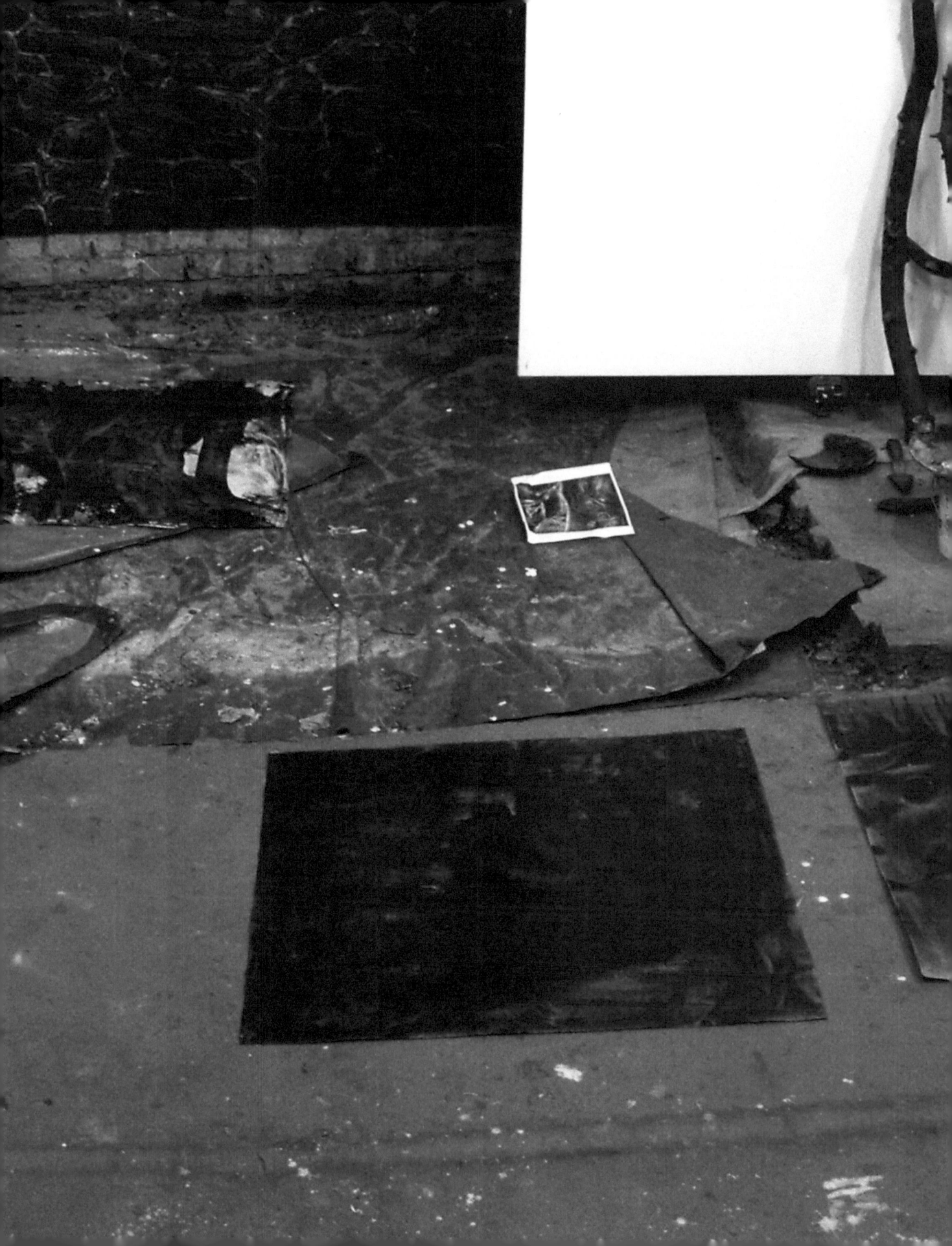

JW: I think it gives a sense of actually standing in front of the monuments, almost like they are bearing down upon you. Weight seems very important.

DPD: I appreciate that comment. I want it to look and feel heavy. I want the weight to represent time and the burden of withstanding time. Sometimes life feels like this. It feels like it could just topple over upon you, and sometimes it does. We, people I mean, can carry so much. These monuments carry a lot as well.

JW: Tell me about your painting process. What kinds of materials are you using other than oil paint?

DPD: I use both oils and acrylics, but sometimes they are just the base. I will mix them with soil, sand, honey, cloth, clay, ink, or whatever suites the subject or texture I'm trying to create. Sometimes the materials are symbolic. Honey was used in the stucco that the Mayans built their monuments with, so I mix it into the painting. I might use soil, or coffee, or clay to create a cracked and broken texture. Sometimes I am surprised by the final results, like the honey I mentioned previously; it still absorbs moisture from the air, and actually sweats from the painting. Luckily, honey is an incredible preservative and is antibacterial. I did get a laugh, however when a bee flew into my house and perched itself by the honey drip on the painting!

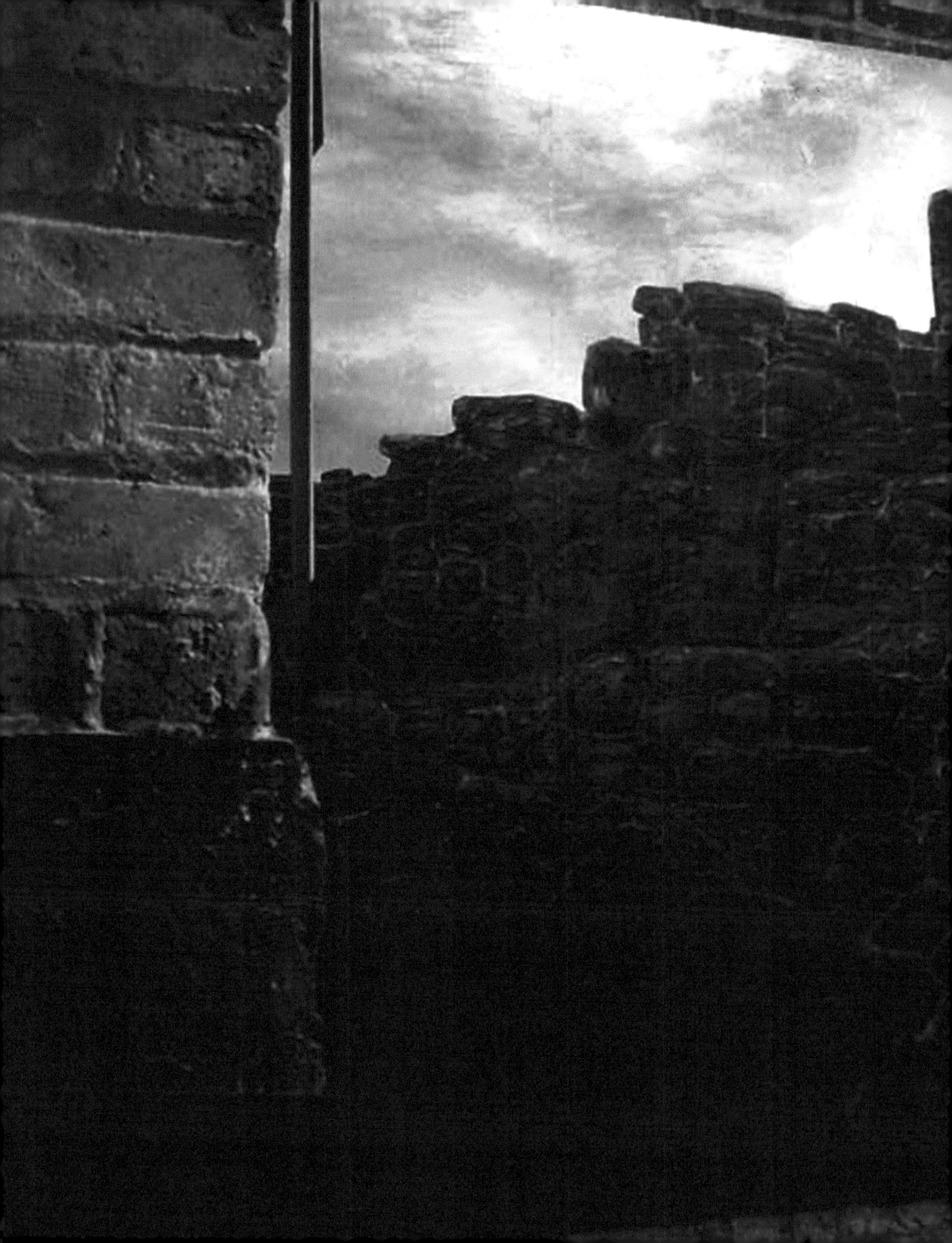

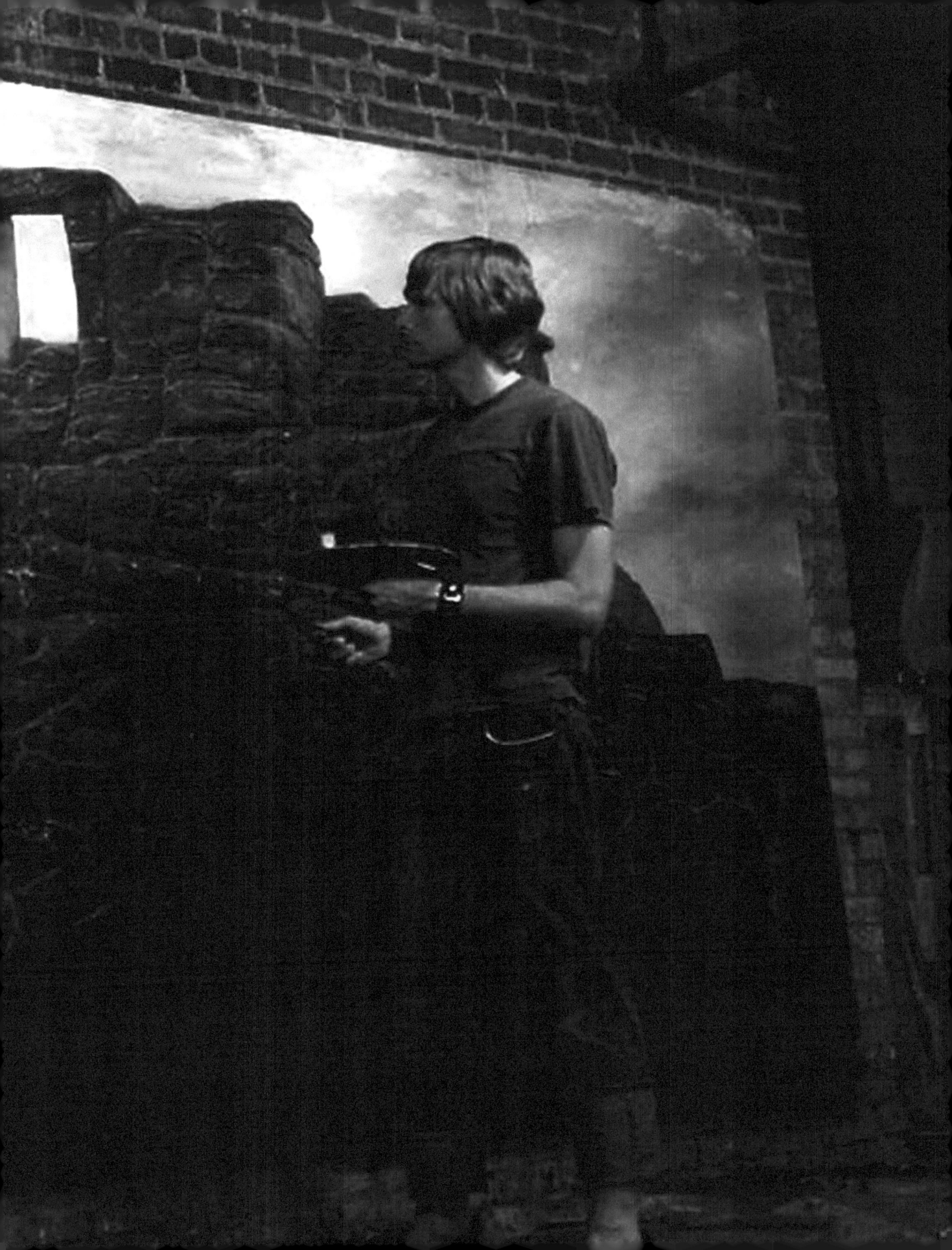

Artist Statement

Disintegrating monuments of the past stand as a testament to the civilizations who built them. Egyptians have the great pyramids, Mayans have ancient temples, the Chinese have their Great Wall... and I, as an American, have no structures to call my own. My art attempts to fill this cultural void by appropriating these relics of the past.

Through painting and photography I recreate the places that call to me from a displaced nostalgia. Focusing on ruins of the near and ancient past, I discuss my need for historical significance. In our era of planned obsolescence and disposable technology, I long for culture and things that came before my time. By collecting historic sites in my art, I can transfer their significance, building a past of my own.

Discovery and documentation are where I always begin. Seeking out artifacts from the past, and photographing them, I capture their presence and translate it onto the canvas either in oil and acrylic paint or by directly transferring the photographic image into the artwork. Using a large surface gives a sense of the monuments original scale, engulfing the viewer. Before bringing the image to life, I lay a loose foundation of drips, washes and textures over the canvas. I rush the surface with acrylics, India ink, and water, building up natural, transparent layers of muted tones. Heavy textures of soil, clay, and other mediums are built upon the canvas and then torn away. Some of the materials are a reflection of the relic, while others are used in a more abstract way. Cracking pieces of clay fall from the fabric of a sky to represent the fragility of time. Soil and ground Coffea Arabica discuss the natural erosion of land and our creations. A mono-chromatic painting palette, leaves room for interpretation and cultivates the imagination of the viewer.

My work continuously reexamines process and technique. I am always evolving my artistic language to create a unique dialogue in my art. This conversation between my work and audience, about culture and historical presence, invites introspection. The art implores the viewer to reclaim the past and explore its implications in a new way by placing familiar and unfamiliar artifacts in new context.

---Solo Exhibitions:
2006 "Age and Decay"
The Lucky Cat, New York, NY

2005 David Paul Downs and Emily Rosen
Dick Blick Gallery, New York, NY

---Selected Group Exhibitions:
2010 "New American Landscape"
Las Manos Gallery, Chicago, IL

2010 "Pocket Change for Global Change Benefit"
Third Coast Comics, Chicago, IL

2010 "The Evidence Against Us"
Las Manos Gallery, Chicago, IL

2009 "die Zeit of Drawing"
Climate/Gallery, New York, NY

2009 "New Works"
Las Manos Gallery, Chicago, IL

2009 "Amnetic State"
7013 Studio, Chicago, IL

2009 "Deck Deck Deck"
APW Gallery, New York, NY

2009 "New Photographs"
Las Manos Gallery, Chicago, IL

2009 "Miriam Benezra Memorial Scholarship Show"
Griffin Gallery, Chicago, IL

2009, 2010 "Edgewater ArtWalk"
Edgewater Storefronts, Chicago, IL

2008 "2nd Annual Square Foot Show"
The Galaxie, Chicago, IL

2005 "Subversive Means"
Dick Blick Gallery, New York, NY

2005 "NoHo ArtWalk",
NoHo Store Fronts, New York, NY

--Published Works:
2010 "New American Landscape" (Sprocketbox Entertainment)
2010 "David Paul Downs: Recent Works" (Sprocketbox Entertainment)
2010 "die Zeit of Drawing" December 2009 Catalogue (Climate/Gallery)
2010 ARTREND NOW! Interview (www.artrendnow.com)

--Awards:
2010 CAAP Grant

Bio
David Downs was born in St. Louis, Missouri in 1978. Throughout his life, David always found escape though artistic means. Since the lack of financial resources kept him from partaking in finer education, most of David's artistic practices have been self-taught. In 1998, David enrolled in St. Louis Community College at Meramec. He brought with him a newly discovered interest in photography, which grew from classes he had taken in high school. David would work as many as three jobs at once while attending Meramec part-time to pursue his education in photography.

David left St. Louis for Chicago, Illinois in 2001. There, with a greater concentration of artists and galleries, David knew Chicago would be the right place to find inspiration. He began to reach beyond photography and wanted to rekindle his love for painting. By experimenting with collage, photo-transfer, and photo-application, David developed many of the techniques he still uses today. In 2004, David moved to New York City to explore it's vast artistic community. In New York, David pushed his medium into bigger and bolder directions. He began to understand his love for texture and how it related to his work as well as how it was reflected his photographs. Throughout New York City, David began showing his work with encouraging success. After a few years, however, it was time to move back to Chicago.

Currently, David is working towards a new aesthetic in his artwork. His work reflects the harmony obtained through diversification and conflict. David now feels that he truly understands the philosophies behind his craft, and his artwork has become stronger and deeper rooted in those beliefs.

Since 2007, David Downs has been teaching adults and children in Chicago the fine art of painting and comic book illustration. He has become well-versed in comic book creation and publication, oil painting, acrylic painting, watercolor, and both traditional and digital photography. His classes can be found through out the city in various schools and venues during the year.